W9-AFS-359

Frederic Chopin

Frederic Chopin

BY FRANZ LISZT

Translated, *with an Introduction, by* EDWARD N. WATERS

MUSIC DIVISION—LIBRARY OF CONGRESS

The Free Press of Glencoe
Collier-Macmillan Ltd., London

FOR INFORMATION, ADDRESS:
The Free Press of Glencoe
A DIVISION OF THE MACMILLAN COMPANY,
THE CROWELL-COLLIER PUBLISHING COMPANY
60 FIFTH AVENUE, NEW YORK 11
COLLIER-MACMILLAN CANADA, LTD., GALT, ONTARIO

DESIGNED BY SIDNEY SOLOMON

LIBRARY OF CONGRESS CATALOG CARD NUMBER: 63–10651

*T*O MY WIFE
LILLY
WHO UNDERSTANDS

Contents*

* Translator's titles

Frederic Chopin

INTRODUCTION

O̲VER A HUNDRED YEARS AGO a book appeared in Paris that was both more and less meaningful than its simple title page implied. It linked together, for neither the first nor the last time, two of the greatest musical names of the century. It was issued in 1852 from the press of M. Escudier, and, as is often the case in our own day, most of it had previously appeared serially in a journal owned by the same publisher (*La France musicale*, February 9 to August 17, 1851). The title was merely *F. Chopin*; the author was simply "F. Liszt." Yet, despite the fame of subject and writer the book is woefully unknown, not only in translation (into several languages) but also in the original French (which, it must be admitted, has few qualities to attract readers).

Chopin died in the French capital during his fortieth year, on October 17, 1849. Liszt, a year younger, was serving as *Kapellmeister* to the court of Weimar. Hearing of his friend's death he evidently determined to create at once a literary portrait of the Polish genius; within a few months he offered it for publication to Breitkopf & Härtel in Leipzig.[1] The German firm was apparently unable to accept it at the moment, and Liszt sent it to the brothers Léon and Marie Escudier, who took it notwithstanding its artificial mannerisms and stylistic awkwardness. Liszt and his strange companion, the Princess Carolyne von Sayn-Wittgenstein, began to receive proofs in January 1851.

Publication followed swiftly in the French magazine (in seventeen installments, but not consecutive issues), and the book, somewhat expanded, was available early in 1852. Rather interesting is the fact that two additional publishers shared the imprint with Escudier: Breitkopf & Härtel, who had already declined it, and Schott of Brussels. Today this edition is a rare volume.

Two English translations were issued in the latter half of the century, by Martha Walker Cook (Philadelphia, 1863) and by John Broadhouse (London, 1899?), but neither was distinguished.

On the continent the book caused no sensation, and not until 1879 did Breitkopf & Härtel bring out a *nouvelle édition*, the text still in French. The original 206 pages, however, had now been stretched to 312, and the enlargement seemed to be only a continuation of the worst fea-

1. Franz Liszt, *Chopin*. Avant-propos d'Alfred Cortot, introduction par J. G. Prod'homme. Paris, 1948, pp. 47ff.

tures of the parent essay. It is doubtless correct to assume that Liszt committed the new edition wholly to the mind and hand of Princess Carolyne, and she yielded willingly to her urge for peroration. The real changes of substance were slight, but much of the material was rearranged and relocated, and the pseudo-philosophy was dismayingly augmented. The Princess found her own literary style and thought irresistible. Even an admirer was forced to admit *"elle corrigeait au courant de la plume les épreuves de ses livres, ajoutant toujours et ne retranchant guère"* ["she corrected the proofs of her books rapidly, always adding and hardly ever subtracting."][2]

La Mara's (Marie Lipsius') German translation, in Liszt's *Gesammelte Schriften,* derives from the bloated *nouvelle édition* and is practically useless in restoring the original version.[3] Not until 1948 was the first authentic French text again readily available, when Corréa of Paris reissued it, edited by J. G. Prod'homme and with a foreword by Alfred Cortot. But it still remains unread and ignored. Why? Probably because a legend of misunderstanding and nonappreciation has grown up around it.

The warmth of the friendship shared by Chopin and Liszt is uncertain. Some historians have called them bosom

2. D. Melegari, "Une amie de Liszt, la Princesse de Sayn Wittgenstein," in *La Revue de Paris,* Sept. 1, 1897, p. 180.

3. The first German translation based upon the edition of 1852 appeared only after the second world war: Franz Liszt, *Frédéric Chopin, nach der neuaufgefundenen Urfassung von 1852 übersetzt von Hans Kühner,* Basel: Amerbach-Verlag, 1948.

companions, others (especially those of more recent date) have insisted that they were far from intimate. Perhaps both views are correct, an early intimacy cooling off as both men were subjected to feminine influence. There can be no doubt that women were disturbing factors in their lives.

Chopin arrived in Paris in the fall of 1831 and first played there on February 26 the following year. Liszt was wholly captivated by his magic. They surely became close friends and mutual admirers at that time. There are several notes from Liszt to Chopin that reveal the original warmth of their relations,[4] and the famous letter[5] they wrote jointly to Hiller shows that the feeling was reciprocal. (This is the document that expresses Chopin's wish that he could steal Liszt's secret of playing his own [Chopin's] *études*.)

Also in Paris, though summering at Croissy, was the lovely Countess Marie d'Agoult, who later became the mother of Liszt's three children. Before chaining Liszt to her she may have looked with favor upon the young Pole. In a letter still little known she begged Chopin to visit her, said she had talked of him to her mother, announced she was not yet recovered from an illness, and declared that *"un de vos nocturnes achèverait de me guérir"* ["one of your nocturnes would complete my cure"]. She was

4. F. F. Chopin, *Correspondance*, Recuellie, revisée, annotée et traduite par Bronislas Edouard Sydow en collaboration avec Suzanne et Denise Chainaye. Paris, 1953–54.
5. Franz Liszt, *Briefe*, ed. La Mara, Leipzig, 1893, Vol. I, No. 6.

so impatient to see him that her postscript read: *"Si vous ne pouvez pas demain, samedi, sinon samedi, dimanche, etc."* ["If you cannot come tomorrow, Saturday, if not Saturday, Sunday, etc."][6] A few weeks later Liszt informs Marie that Chopin has been quite ill, and she offers her summer home as a place to recuperate. It will be excellent as a *maison de santé* [sanatorium]; there will be fresh air, delicious milk, and the music of nightingales. Moreover, she admires his astonishing *études* and hopes they will soon meet again.[7]

Even years afterward (November 9, 1838) Marie wrote to a friend and said of Chopin: *"C'est le seul pianiste que je puisse entendre non seulement sans ennui, mais avec un profond recueillement"* ["He is the only pianist I can listen to not only free of boredom, but with a deep composure"].[8] Presumably Liszt never saw these words.

Then in the fall of 1836, at a literary gathering in his own quarters, Liszt introduced to Chopin the formidable but unforgettable George Sand (Aurore Dudevant). The Pole disliked her at once and had no hesitation in saying so. As he and Hiller walked home after the party he spoke of the antipathy Sand had aroused and expressed doubts that she was really a woman. And when he wrote to his family in Warsaw he said her face was not sympathetic, was displeasing, and that he actually felt repelled.[9]

6. Chopin, *Correspondance*, II, 87.
7. *Ibid.*, II, 94–95.
8. *Ibid.*, II, 262.
9. *Ibid.*, II, 208.

Only a short time passed, however, and Chopin entertained some friends (Liszt among them) on December 13, 1836; one of his guests was the lady from Nohant. He still disliked her, but her interest in him was obvious from the costume she wore that evening, a gown of white and red, the colors of Chopin's native land.[10]

At last Chopin's resistance was completely overcome, and he and Sand embarked upon an affair that lasted for some years. As it developed, however, Marie d'Agoult seemed exceedingly annoyed. Surely she wanted Chopin's homage, surely she felt great satisfaction in gaining the dedication of the *Études*, Op. 25 (published 1837), and almost as surely she was vexed as she watched the relations of Sand and Chopin advance to a point that removed all doubt of their significance. But Marie could do little beyond affect complete indifference. She and Liszt were together, and she posed as a warm friend of Sand. In her letters to George, however, she could not resist the temptation of penning sly and malicious references to Chopin which barely veiled a hurt pride and a degree of spite.

The two ladies unfortunately had a mutual friend, Countess Carlotta Marliani, and her favorite pastime seems to have been to tell George and Marie what each thought of the other. Soon, therefore, George placed Marie in a novel, *Horace* (published 1841), where she was known as the Vicomtesse de Chailly. The portrait was far from flattering. This pseudo-fictional character was terrifyingly thin,

10. *Ibid.*, II, 209.

had doubtful teeth and dry skin, was arrogant and over-loaded with rings, and had a purchased title: "in short, her nobility was as artificial as everything else about her—teeth, bosom, and heart."[11] It is understandable that George and Marie ceased to be friends, and even later when their quarrel was patched up, their relations lacked the warmth of earlier days.

As this unpleasantness developed, Liszt was already on his extensive concert tours. In writing to him Marie was sharply critical of Chopin and Sand, and Franz had to side and sympathize with her. He admitted that she had been placed in *Horace*, but he advised her to be calm and to appear unaffected. Her rejoinder to this was rather strange: "I am neither upset nor embittered by it. . . . You know very well that I can only be hurt in one way. Since she has not succeeded in winning your love, she can-not harm me."[12]

In this peculiar situation Chopin seems to have been an innocent victim. As Marie and George became more embroiled, since Chopin was clearly (even if unwittingly) involved, Liszt could scarcely maintain with him the friendly relations of former days. Besides, his constant traveling made social intercourse physically impossible. Chopin seemed ignored, and over a period of nearly five years no letter from Liszt to Marie mentions the Polish composer in any way.[13]

11. André Maurois, *Lélia*, Paris, 1952, p. 341.
12. Franz Liszt, *F. Chopin* (Prod'homme), Paris, 1948, p. 39.
13. *Ibid.*, p. 39.

Chopin and Liszt were probably somewhat jealous of each other, which should also occasion no surprise. Each was uniquely gifted; each knew he could do things the other could not; each may have aspired to accomplishments reserved only for the other. In 1840 Ernest Legouvé, French critic and *littérateur*, wrote Liszt a letter that sheds some light on this matter:

. . . Schoelcher told me that an article of mine on Chopin, in which I placed him above you, had been painful to you: since my musical opinion has only an individual value, I can not attribute to vanity the slight resentment you expressed to Schoelcher; it can only be the sorrow of a friend seeing himself attacked, so to speak, through a friend, and this is so touching that I feel the need of explaining and justifying myself. . . .

I shall not affront you by retracting and saying: I let that sentence escape in the first reaction to an unguarded admiration; no, since I wrote it I thought it. But here is why. In the arts, it seems to me, first place belongs to unity, to that which is complete. I believe Chopin to be complete; performance and composition, everything in him is in harmony and of equal value; . . . Chopin has reached the realization of his ideal. You, on the contrary, and I have heard you say this, are only halfway in your development . . . the pianist has arrived, but the composer is perhaps delayed. . . . I tell you this, and I sincerely believe it, the day when the inward Liszt comes out, the day when that amazing power of execution has its counterpart and its complement equally in composition (and that day is perhaps not far off, for men like you grow), on that day you will not be called the first pianist of Europe, you will be called by another name! So bear me no grudge! If you still do not satisfy me completely, it is because I see more in you than the others, that is what I wait for, what I hope for, what I believe.[14]

It is obvious that Liszt had his moments of petulance, but Chopin was no less frail. Legouvé again paints the scene:

> He [Chopin] had asked me to review [his public concert], Liszt claimed that honor. I hastened to give this good news to Chopin, who said to me quietly:
> "I should have preferred that it be you."
> "You cannot think that, my dear friend! An article by Liszt is a stroke of good fortune for the public and for you. Believe in his admiration for your talent. I promise you that he will make you a beautiful kingdom."
> "Yes," he replied, smiling, "within his own empire."[15]

Chopin's concert was presented on April 26, 1841; Liszt's review was for the *Revue et Gazette musicale de Paris*, May 2, 1841. Admirers of Chopin and detractors of Liszt cite it as an illustration of Liszt's pique or jealousy. It is difficult to see why. Legouvé was quite right in calling the article charming and sympathetic.[16] The concert was important socially and musically, and Liszt was journalistically justified in stressing both aspects.

Chopin played only his own compositions, of course, including several *Préludes, Mazurkas,* two *Polonaises* (Op. 40), the second *Ballade,* and the third *Scherzo.*[17] Liszt's

14. La Mara, *Briefe hervorragender Zeitgenossen an Franz Liszt,* Leipzig, 1895, I, 12–14.
15. E. Legouvé, *Soixante ans de souvenirs,* Paris, 1888, II, 161–62.
16. *Ibid.*
17. Chopin, *Correspondance* (Sydow), I, xliv; Edouard Ganche, *Frédéric Chopin,* Paris, 1926, p. 255.

criticism, it is true, emphasized Chopin's position and uniqueness in art rather than the performance of a particular evening, but such an approach is the privilege of any guest reviewer:

Last Monday evening at eight o'clock the salons of M. Pleyel were brilliantly lighted; a ceaseless stream of carriages deposited at the foot of the steps, carpeted and decked with fragrant flowers, the most elegant ladies, the most fashionable young men, the most famous artists, the richest financiers, the most illustrious lords, the élite of society—a complete aristocracy of birth, wealth, talent and beauty.

An open grand piano was on a platform; crowding around, people vied for the closest seats; composing themselves in anticipation, they would not miss a chord, a note, an intention, a thought of him who was about to sit there. And they were right to be so greedy, attentive, and religiously wrought up, for the one they waited for, the one they wanted to see, hear, admire, and applaud was not only a skilled virtuoso, a pianist expert in the playing of notes—he was not only an artist of great renown—he was all this and much more, he was Chopin.

Coming to France some ten years ago Chopin, in the throng of pianists then swarming from everywhere, struggled for neither first nor second place. He was rarely heard in public; the essentially poetic nature of his talent was out of place there. Like those flowers that only release their fragrance in the night, he needed an atmosphere of peace and calm to display freely the treasure of melody resting in him. Music was his language, the divine language in which he expressed a whole series of feelings that only a few could understand. As with that other great poet, Mickiewicz, his friend and compatriot, the muse of the fatherland inspired his songs, and the laments of Poland lent to his tones a strange and mysterious poesy which, for those who have truly felt it, is like nothing else at all. If his name is less brilliant, if the aureole around his head less bright, it was not that the same energy of thought perhaps was wanting or the same depth of feeling shown by the gifted author of *Konrad Wallenrod* and the *Pèlerins;* but his means of expression were too limited, his instrument too imperfect. With the piano he could not be completely self-revealed. Hence, if we mistake not, a numb and ceaseless suffering, a certain reluctance to outward communication, a sadness concealed beneath a show of gaiety—a complete individuality, indeed, remarkable and engaging to the last degree.

As we have said, only rarely, at very long intervals, was Chopin heard in public. But what would have led any other, almost certainly, to be forgotten and obscured, was exactly what assured him a reputation above the whim of fashion and protected him from rivalries, jealousies and injustice. Chopin, set apart from the violent turmoil that, for some years, thrusts one against or over another, has been steadily surrounded by faithful disciples, enthusiastic pupils and warm friends who, shielding him from vexing clashes and painful contacts, have not ceased to spread his works as well as admiration for his genius and respect for his name. Thus, this celebrity, delicate, high-minded, surpassingly aristocratic, has remained free of all attack. Around him criticism is wholly silent, as if posterity had claimed him. And in the brilliant audience that flocked to the poet too long mute there was no restraint, no holding back; all mouths shouted united praise.

We shall not undertake here a detailed analysis of Chopin's compositions. Without artificial striving for originality he has been himself, both in style and conception. To new thoughts he has been able to give new form. The wild and rugged elements of his country have found expression in bold dissonance, in strange harmonies, while the delicacy and grace of his nature are revealed in a thousand turns of phrase, in a thousand ornaments of inimitable fancy.

In Monday's concert Chopin had chosen by preference those of his works farthest removed from the classical forms. He played neither concerto nor sonata nor fantasy nor variations, but préludes, études, nocturnes and mazurkas. Speaking to a society rather than to a public, he could safely show himself as what he is—a poet, elegiac, profound, chaste and dreaming. He had no need to astonish or to shock; he sought delicate sympathy rather than noisy acclaim. Let us say at once that this sympathy was not lacking. With the very first chords he established an intimate communication between himself and his audience. Two études and a ballade had to be repeated, and but for fear of increasing the fatigue already obviously betrayed in his pale countenance, the crowd would have demanded again every piece on the program.

The Préludes of Chopin are quite special compositions. They are not merely pieces, as the title might suggest, intended to be played as an introduction to other pieces—they are poetic preludes, like those of a great contemporary poet which lull the soul in golden dreams and raise it to ideal realms. Admirable in their variety, they contain a skill and substance that are appreciated only after careful study. The music is spontaneous, brilliant and fresh. They have the freedom and spaciousness characteristic of works of genius.

What can be said of the mazurkas, those little masterpieces so whimsical yet so highly finished?

A faultless sonnet equals a long poem, said a man who wielded authority in the finest century of French letters. We are tempted to apply the exaggeration of this axiom to the mazurkas and to say that we, at least, find many of them the equal of *very long* operas. . . .

The fame or success that crowns talent or genius is partly owing to fortunate circumstances. Lasting triumphs are, in truth, seldom unfair. Since justice, however, is possibly the rarest quality of the human mind, it happens that some artists achieve success within, others outside the confines of, their true worth. It is well known that in the ebb and flow of the tides, a tenth wave comes that is stronger than the others; so it is in the world—there are men, swept along by this tenth wave of fortune, who go higher and farther than others who may be their equals or even their superiors. The genius of Chopin has not been helped by special circumstances. His success, though very great, has remained within his claims. But, and we say this emphatically, he need envy no one. The noblest, most genuine satisfaction that the artist can experience, is it not to feel himself above his fame, superior to his success, even greater than his glory?

This was praise indeed, notwithstanding certain qualifications, but Chopin did not like it, and he must have unveiled his feelings to his family. On December 30, 1841, his father in Warsaw wrote the following to his sensitive son: "One thing I'm curious about is to know whether you have seen Liszt since his article and whether you are together as you used to be. It would be a pity if there were a cooling of your friendship."[18] But the cooling undoubtedly happened, and apparently much to Liszt's unhappiness. In Posen on February 26, 1843, Liszt sent a

18. Mieczyslaw Karlowicz, *Souvenirs inédits de Frédéric Chopin*, Paris, 1904, p. 95.

note to Chopin which the critic Rellstab would deliver. After introducing the bearer, Liszt continued the message to his *"cher ancien ami"* (addressing him with the intimate *tu*): "I am especially anxious to send greetings and to seize this occasion to repeat again, at the risk of appearing monotonous, that my affection and admiration for you will always be the same, and that you can always make use of me in any way whatever."[19] There seems to be no evidence that Chopin responded to this approach, and for all practical purposes the two artists had no further relations.

As the years went by, the lives of both altered radically. Chopin's health steadily worsened, he broke with George Sand, and he died on October 17, 1849. Liszt became ever more glamorous as he developed into history's greatest pianist. His strange romance with Marie d'Agoult ended, he voluntarily abandoned concertizing, he met his second woman of destiny (the Princess Carolyne von Sayn-Wittgenstein, of Polish descent), and he established himself at Weimar as court *Kapellmeister*. He retained, nevertheless, a keen interest in Chopin and clamored for news of any changes in his colleague's existence. Even from Woronince, Carolyne's eastern home near Kiev, Liszt wrote to Marie (February 10, 1847) asking if the break between Chopin and Sand was final, and he requested all the details.[20] Nothing could be more natural.

When Chopin died, Liszt was profoundly affected.

19. *Ibid.*, p. 174.
20. Liszt, *Chopin* (Prod'homme), p. 40.

He had been intimately associated with the Polish genius, and he certainly appreciated Chopin's artistic uniqueness. It is not unreasonable to suppose that he deeply regretted any incidents that drew them apart. Why not write a book as a tribute to his onetime friend? Three considerations possibly encouraged this idea. To the world of music Liszt was already well known as an interesting author; Carolyne was Polish and would stimulate a literary tribute to a celebrated compatriot; it was rumored that Albert Grzymala (a close friend of Chopin) was about to write a biography.[21] Circumstances and feelings were irresistible: the book had to be done.

Curiously enough, though the book appeared under Liszt's name, the amount of his authorship is unknown. In fact, the amount of any of his authorship is unknown, for there seems to be good reason for doubting that he wrote any of the essays to which his name is attached,[22] and we have the phenomenal situation (or possibility) of a great musician issuing reams of material not a word of which came from his own pen! Marie d'Agoult is charged as being his first ghost writer, Carolyne Wittgenstein the second. Both women became prolific authors in their own right after serving this apprenticeship, but why they were willing to work in such obscurity remains an unanswered riddle.

Haraszti indicates that Liszt at least consulted and

21. *Ibid.*, p. 43.
22. Emile Haraszti, "Die Autorschaft der literarischen Werke Franz Liszts," in *Ungarische Jahrbücher*, XXI (Nov. 1941), 173–236.

possibly collaborated with the Princess. If this be true, he may have acted in self-defense. "Her" *Chopin* is written for the most part in execrable French, turgid, long-winded, and bombastic (the second edition is worse). Liszt was worried about the literary style and rightly so. Years later Carolyne's writing was criticized as a "literary tower of Babel . . . German written in French . . . a translation, indeed, by a Pole who really did not understand the original."[23] These literary defects may have aroused suspicion, even during her lifetime, about the authorship of the Chopin book. Questioned on this point, she merely smiled and replied: "When two beings have so completely merged, can it ever be said where the work of one begins or the other ends?"[24] But with his name on the title page Liszt assumed responsibility for the book and its contents.

He set about his task in the most approved way—by sending an elaborate questionnaire to Louise Iedrzeiewicz (Chopin's sister, still in Paris after her brother's funeral) less than a month after Chopin's death:

> Madame,
>   My long friendship with your brother, the sincere and deep admiration I always held for him as for one of the noblest glories of our art, force upon me, as it were, the obligation of issuing a few pages to honor his memory. They will probably form a brochure of 3 to 4 folios. In order to give this work all desirable accuracy, allow me to affirm to you my intimate relations with the illustrious

23. Melegari, *op. cit.*, p. 179.
24. *Ibid.*, p. 168.

deceased, and to submit several questions relating to his biography. I should be infinitely grateful if you will kindly put the answers in the margin.

My secretary M. Bellini [i.e., Belloni], who has the honor of bearing these lines to you, is likewise charged to bring me your response as quickly as possible.

Please accept, Madame, my most respectful and devoted greetings.   F. Liszt.[25]

Pilsen, November 14, 1849

It would appear that Liszt received no reply to this appeal,[26] although the contrary has sometimes been assumed. Louise may have been prejudiced from the outset —by her brother's earlier discomfiture, by Liszt's haste in dispatching the queries, by some of the points they touch upon. She handed the questionnaire to Jane Stirling, Chopin's Scottish pupil, who wrote the answers that presumably satisfied Louise. It is doubtful that Liszt ever saw them.

The questionnaire, a curious document in twelve sections, is given below, together with the answers:

Question 1

The date and place of his birth.

Question 2

What was his childhood like? Is there any relevant anecdote or circumstance characteristic of his taste and habits' during that period?

Answers 1 and 2

The 1st and 2nd questions can only be answered by the memories of his mother, who is still living. The

25. Karlowicz, *op. cit.*, pp. 200 ff. (including questionnaire and answers).

26. Haraszti, *op. cit.*, p. 227.

recollections of Chopin's contemporaries are not adequate to satisfy fully these two queries.

Question 3

When did his musical gifts begin to appear, and what were his first studies? Were they difficult for him? Was he accustomed to improvise at an early age?

Answer 3

His very first piano study disclosed his extraordinary musical gifts. In approaching the principles of harmony he seemed to be recalling a forgotten skill rather than learning it for the first time. Because of his physical frailty, perhaps, improvisation fatigued him less than written composition, the purity of which never came up to the demands of his exquisite taste.

Question 4

In what college or school was he placed? Are the names remembered of some of his classmates whom he liked the most? Was not his musical talent already very well known and appreciated at that time? Was he not often invited by his friends' parents, who were charmed by his talent and his mind? In visiting homes did he not often go, about 1824, to that of Princess Czetwertynska whose sons were his schoolmates? Did he visit Princess Lowicz and other great salons of Warsaw?

Answer 4

His father, a very learned man, was connected with the University of Warsaw which, during Chopin's education, had professors of high distinction. The training at home had already developed his aptitudes in a remarkable way. All his schoolmates were very fond of him. Throughout his life he retained a lasting memory of them, and all who were able to see him

again in Paris can testify to the eagerness with which
he sought to renew the former intimacy and to recall
the memories of youth. His precocious talent opened
Warsaw's great salons to him. Even the Grand Duke
Constantine and his wife took a keen pleasure in
following the astonishing development of the marvelous child.

Question 5

Was he involved in any way in the Revolution of
1830? Where was he in November 1830 and during the following year? For what reason did he then
depart from Poland? Did he leave his father and
mother there? Did he maintain relations with them
thereafter? Where did he then go upon leaving the
country and what were his plans? How many concerts did he give in Vienna and Munich, and what
was his purpose in giving them? Was this the first
time he was heard in public or the first time that he
gave concerts?

Answer 5

He was never involved in any of his country's political events. He had already left Poland in November 1830, and he never returned there afterward. He
was too good a Pole to separate from his proscribed
brothers. But as a devoted son this separation from
his family caused him great suffering. Death snatched
his father away 4 years ago, and he never ceased
to mourn him with tears flowing from the inexhaustible spring of his heart in tender memory of the
domestic hearth. Then, as today, his sister Louise
rushed the hundreds of leagues to lavish on him, with
sublime affection, the solicitude that no weariness
could weaken. Chopin gave several concerts before
leaving Warsaw, and did the same in traveling from
Vienna to Paris. But the greatest success of his con-

certs could never overcome his dislike for this manner of exploiting his talent. His genius needed more positive reaction than a nondescript public usually evinces. It comes with vague demands and preconceived preferences; it understands with difficulty anything off the beaten track; it makes the artist or the poet descend to its level rather than rising to their height. Moreover, the kind of effect produced by the intimate character not only of the works of Chopin's mind but also of his marvelous playing could not bear the glaring light of halls of exhibition.

Question 6

What Polish families did he cultivate the most during his stay in Paris? Of what friends was he fondest during his last days?

My intimate association with Chopin gives me the right, perhaps, to ask you a few question on his relations with Mme Sand?

I should like some details on his trip to the island of Majorca and the impression he retained from it. What time of his life left him the sweetest memory? And in his final moments what persons remained dearest in his thoughts?

Answer 6

All the Polish families living in Paris loved him dearly. He was welcome everywhere, from the *Hôtel Lambert* to the most humble abode. And for 3 days of his holy agony all these families knelt at the foot of his bed, commingling their tears and their sorrows. Such a death, more than all else, determines opinion on a life.

Question 7

What was the nature of his connection with Mme Sand toward the end? Can it be believed that the

romance of *Lucrezia Floriani* with the prince, said to
be the story of their intimate relations, is true?

Answer 7

The intimate life of Ch. was, for him, a sanc-
tuary equally intimate. Ch. was too sparing of details to give them room in his biography. During his
journey to the island of Majorca he fell gravely ill,
and afterward his strength was never able to return
to normal. Inevitably his spirits, formerly so bright,
reacted to this more and more and day by day. He
was too lofty and too refined to be willing to see
himself in the prince-hero's allusions in the novel
Lucrezia Floriani, and he exercised so much delicacy
and integrity in all his relations that it would be very
difficult to follow the intimate disclosures thereof.

Question 8

Did he share Mme Sand's ultra-democratic opinions?
Was he interested in the cause she supported? What
were his relations with Louis Blanc, Ledru-Rollin,
and other celebrities of Mme Sand's circle?

Answer 8

His political opinions never had anything in common with the exaggerations of the persons mentioned;
he made no propaganda and none was exerted upon
him—it could have had no effect. He had too clear
a mind to fail to sense the evils of the time, too
great a heart to remain indifferent to them, and too
much judgment to become entangled in any kind of
political unrest.

Question 9

Had he already broken his association with her in
1848? And can the causes of this break be determined? Was it furious or friendly? Did he suffer
from it or was it easy for him? Did he often stay at
Nohant, and did he find the visits pleasant?

Answer 9

It would appear that the marriage of Mme Sand's daughter made this period rather difficult for a mother so that Chopin's stay at Nohant could not continue without serious drawbacks. The daughter was reverently present at his death. The mother was not in Paris. He did not speak of her in his last hours.

Question 10

Why did he go to London in 1848? How long did he stay there? Why did he return? Is the anecdote authentic that was told me by M. Schlesinger, about the lessons he gave to Queen Victoria who came to take them in Chopin's quarters since he was too ill to go out?

Answer 10

Drawn to England by some friends, he stayed there 8 months, but the climate was fatal for him. He never told anything extraordinary about his relations with the high personage of that country, except they were markedly kind to him.

Question 11

From what year dates his chest affliction? How were his spirits in his final moments? Did he regret life? Did he watch death's approach with terror? When did he stop composing? Did he express the desire to write more when he could no longer do so? Does he leave any unfinished works, and of what kind?

Answer 11

The autopsy showed nothing on the basic cause of death. The chest seemed to be less involved than the heart. It was the death of a soul pure, resigned, and believing. Not the slightest cloud from beyond the tomb came to darken his final moments. All his features reposed in the confidence of faith and love.

He left clear directions that condemned his unpublished compositions to the flames.

Question 12

How were his final moments? Is it true that, as reported by the music journals, he asked to be dressed in his concert costume when he felt death approaching?

Did he receive the last rites? Did he ask for them or refuse them? And what priest came to his bed as he lay dying?

Answer 12

To have seen Chopin only once in his life is enough to have believed him incapable of the smallness of mind to worry about the choice of garb for awaiting death. He received it like a good Catholic, having made all his devotions under the guidance and through the attentions of his old friend, the Abbé Jelowicki.

Miss Stirling's comments were of no use if Liszt never saw them, but his questions are still important. They show what he wished to emphasize. Some critics have declared that they reveal a great ignorance of Chopin the man, that they refute Liszt's claims of an earlier intimacy. This can hardly be sustained. When they were friendliest they were both youths in their twenties—and young men of that age waste little time discussing families, childhood, and schooling. Liszt was, perhaps, indiscreet in asking so many questions about George Sand, but he had brought Chopin and Sand together. Who had a better right to know? (After all, Liszt was only thirty-eight when he penned the questions, and with all his sophistication he still had a lot to learn about life.)

Evidently the book was written with no help from Chopin's family. But Liszt was obviously disturbed by its form or style or both, and he sought help and reassurance. He sent the manuscript (his or Carolyne's—it has not been preserved) to Joseph d'Ortigue, French musicologist, and asked for criticism. When it came he wrote his thanks (April 24, 1850):

> I am truly grateful to you, dear friend, for kindly taking the trouble of devoting a few hours to reading my manuscript of *Chopin*, in spite of the pressure of your own affairs. The welcome judgment you offer on three fourths of my work is highly flattering encouragement, and I thank you warmly for the observations you make on the fourth fourth. I shall not fail to profit from them.[27]

Unfortunately Liszt also sent the manuscript to the great critic Sainte-Beuve, asking for similar assistance, but here he was turned down. The reply was friendly enough, yet there was no doubt of Sainte-Beuve's opinion of the product:

Paris, March 31, 1850
Dear Friend,

> You cannot doubt that I would have done the little revision you requested with the greatest alacrity if it had been physically possible. But since my return from Belgium to Paris, I have been living here in working conditions so constricting and demanding that it is impossible for me to steal a single moment. From glancing over your interesting and generous appreciation it would be necessary, it seems to me, in order to cast it into French as I understand it, to begin again and recopy the entire work,

27. Liszt, *Chopin* (Prod'homme), pp. 47–48.

and I am in no condition at the moment to undertake this. Believe, dear friend, in my sincere regret, in the memory I keep of all your kind feelings for me, and in the feelings with which I should like to prove to you that I am ever your

Ste. Beuve[28]

The faults of the book are surely and primarily owing to the Princess. Its wordiness, its obfuscations, its ramblings on Polish nobility, on national traits, on the glories of the aristocratic spirit, on the value of Polish dances in their original vigor—all of these excursions away from Chopin and his music must be laid at her door. Page after page after page is devoted to fanciful improvisation, and the reader (far from being entertained) wonders when he will again encounter the composer hidden behind all this verbiage. Prod'homme was certainly right in suggesting that Carolyne, an indefatigable talker, wrote as she spoke, and that some of these pages must have been her monologue alone.[29] Haraszti was no less right in declaring the book to be often *ungeniessbar*.[30] Yet it contains many sensible things, and we today can only hope that these are the sentiments that Liszt insisted be included.

Liszt closed his book by adding a few pages of general sentiment expressing his grief and by re-emphasizing the high place that Chopin would hold in music history. Thus terminated the public tribute from one great artist to

28. La Mara, *op. cit.*, I, No. 94.
29. Liszt, *Chopin* (Prod'homme), p. 59.
30. Haraszti, *op. cit.*, p. 228.

another. It is regrettable, perhaps, that Liszt more than once referred to the book as a biography. This it is not, at least in the ordinary sense of the word. It is not scholarly and it is not accurate; the author's memory was faulty, and he evidently had little patience for research. For the main facts of Chopin's life a standard biography is essential. In this new edition I have formulated chapter titles to assist the reader.

Liszt's product is, rather, an appreciation, a memoir, a revelation of much of Liszt's reaction to Chopin's music in the mid-nineteenth century. It is a testimonial by an artist who knew the feelings and the person he was writing about. That he exaggerated or was led into exaggeration, that he digressed or was led into digression should not blind present-day readers and students of history to its real merit—warm, generous, and imaginative praise of a friend and colleague whose death was surely an "irreparable loss."

1

MUSIC AND INNOVATIONS

*H*owever lamented he may be by all artists and persons who knew him, we doubt that the time has yet come for him (so deeply mourned and fully appreciated) to hold the high position of universal regard that the future likely reserves as his.

If, as has often been proven, *no man is a prophet in his own land,* is it not also known that prophets, men who sense the future and announce it by their work, are not acknowledged as such in their own age? Moreover, it would be venturesome to say that the situation can be otherwise. Young generations of artists protest vainly against the laggards whose invariable custom is to strike at the living through the dead. It is time alone, in music as in other arts, that can sometimes reveal complete beauty and full worth.

Since the many forms of art are only varied incantations destined to arouse sentiments and passions and make them, as it were, perceptible and tangible, since they communicate the quickenings of emotion, genius appears through the design of new shapes now and again adapted to feelings not yet embraced within the magic circle. Can it be hoped that, in those arts combining sensation with emotion unaided by thought and reflection, the very introduction of uncommon forms and styles is not already an obstacle to the immediate grasp of a work? Do not surprise and even exhaustion, caused by the strangeness of unfamiliar impressions, produce for the masses the novelty of an unknown tongue which at first seems to be uncivilized? The mere burden of accustoming the ear to it will discourage many who stubbornly refuse to study it. People of great vitality and youthfulness, those least enslaved by habit which is so respectable to its victims, are the first to be curious about, then to acquire a passion for, the new idiom. Through them it enters and takes over the resisting segments of the public which at last grasps its meaning, scope, and construction, and does justice to the qualities or riches it may enfold. Thus musicians who are not bound to conventional routines need the help of time more than other artists. They cannot hope that death will bring to their works that instantaneous *plus value* given to those of painters. None, to make his manuscripts more profitable, could revive the trick of a great Flemish master who, while living, wished to exploit his future glory by charging his wife to spread the report of his death to make more dear his canvases with which he had thoughtfully adorned his studio.

Whatever be the popularity, therefore, of certain creations of him who was broken by suffering long before his end, it is nonetheless likely that posterity will grant his works a regard less frivolous and less light than they now attract. Those subsequently concerned with the history of music will determine his rôle there, surely a great one, distinguished by such rare melodic genius, by such happy and remarkable expansions of harmonic texture, that his triumphs will rightly supersede many a work of greater extent though it be played and replayed by great orchestras, sung and resung by a swarm of *prime donne*.

By restricting himself to the limiting compass of the piano Chopin, we think, demonstrated one of the most essential qualities of a writer: the true appreciation of the medium wherein his excellence lies. And yet this fact, in our opinion a great merit, damaged the extent of his fame. It might have been difficult for another, possessed of such lofty melodic and harmonic skills, to resist the temptations presented by the singing bow, the languorous flute, the stormy orchestra, and the deafening trumpet which we steadfastly believe to be the only messenger of the ancient goddess courted for quick favors. What deliberate conviction he must have had to limit himself to a seemingly more barren plot and through his genius to bring forth there something apparently incapable of blooming on this soil! What intuitive penetration does this excluding choice disclose which, snatching certain instrumental effects from their usual domain where the noisy froth would be trampled underfoot, transfers them into a more restricted but more idealized sphere? What instinctive confidence in the future power of his instrument must have ordered this deliberate abandonment of a practicality so widely accepted! Any other would doubtless have considered wrong this removal of such great thoughts from their customary interpreters! How sincerely must we admire this sole preoccupation with beauty for its own sake. It preserved his talent from the common urge to divide each bit of melody among some hundred desks, and it caused him to expand the resources of art by teaching their concentration in a lesser space.

Far from aspiring to orchestral tumult, Chopin was content to see his thought completely reproduced on the ivory of the keyboard, achieving his aim of no loss in power, without claim upon ensemble effects and minus the scene-painter's brush. The value of the drawings from this delicate pencil has received too little serious and attentive reflection. Today it is the custom to consider great only those composers who have left a half-dozen operas, as many oratorios, and a few symphonies—they are asked to do everything and a little more than everything. But the rightness of this idea, however generally entertained, is nonetheless highly questionable. We are far from disputing the glory, more difficult to attain, and the real superiority of epic singers who reveal their splendid creations in a broad frame. Yet we should like to apply to music that value which is attached to material proportions in other branches of the fine arts and which, in painting for example, places a canvas of twenty inches square—like *la Vision d'Ézéchiel* or *le Cimitière* of Ruys-Daël [*sic*]—among masterpieces considered more costly than a picture of huge dimension though it be by a Rubens or a Tintoretto. In literature is Béranger less a great poet for having compressed his thought within the narrow limits of the song? Does not Petrarch owe his triumph to his *Sonnets,* and among those who have most often repeated their sweet rhymes, are many even aware of his poem on Africa? Slowly disappearing, we are sure, are the preconceptions still opposing an artist who has produced only sonatas like Franz Schubert's and disputing his creative superiority over another who has scored the dull airs of so many operas which need not be mentioned. Likewise in music, in compositions of all kinds, there will come full appreciation of the eloquence and talent that express thoughts and feelings regardless of scope and means of interpretation.

Now, an intelligent analysis of Chopin's works cannot be made without disclosing beauties of a very high order, a wholly new expression, and a harmonic structure as original as it is learned. Here boldness always justifies itself; richness, even exuberance, does not suppress clarity; uniqueness does not sink to baroque eccentricity. The chasings are not undisciplined, and the luxury of ornament does not overburden the elegance of leading lines. His best works abound in combinations which, it may be said, are epoch-making in the treatment of musical style. Daring, brilliant, seductive, they conceal their depth beneath so much grace, their skill beneath so much charm

33

that it is difficult to withdraw sufficiently from their captive hold to judge them coolly from the standpoint of theoretic value. The latter has already been sensed, but it will be increasingly recognized when the time comes for a careful examination of the services rendered to art during the period when Chopin was active.

We owe to him the extension of chords, be they struck together, arpeggiated, or rolled; those chromatic and enharmonic twisting lines, of which his pages offer such striking examples; those little groups of embellishing notes, over the melodic figure, that fall like drops of iridescent dew. He gave to this type of ornament, originating solely in the *fioritures* of the great and venerated school of Italian song, the elements of surprise and variety beyond the capacity of the human voice which, until then, had been slavishly imitated by the piano in stereotyped and monotonous decoration. He invented those admirable harmonic progressions that lent a serious stamp even to pages seeming to have no claim to such importance because of the lightness of their subject. But what matters the subject? Is it not, rather, its flashing idea, its pulsating emotion, that heightens, ennobles, and augments it? What sadness, subtlety, and shrewdness, above all what *art* are in the masterpieces of La Fontaine, with *subjects* so common and titles so modest. The *Études* and the *Préludes* are similar—yet the pieces of Chopin bearing these titles will remain no less types of perfection in a style (springing like all his works from the nature of his poetic genius) that he created. Almost his earliest productions, they bear the impress of a youthful verve that fades in some of his later writings, more elaborate, more detailed, and more contrived, then vanishes completely from his final works, which show an overexcited sensibility that might be called the effort of exhaustion.

If we had to speak here in academic terms of the development of piano music, we would dissect those magnificent pages that offer so rich a harvest of observations. First of all we would explore those *Nocturnes, Ballades, Impromptus,* and *Scherzos,* all filled with harmonic refinements as unfamiliar as they are unexpected. We would seek them similarly in his *Polonaises, Mazurkas, Valses,* and *Boléros.* But this is no time or place for such labor; it is of interest only to those skilled in counterpoint and figured bass.

The sentiment flowing from these works, highly romantic and individual, has made them popular and carried them far. They bear their author's stamp and yet they are sympathetic, not only to that country which he again distinguishes but to all who could ever feel the misery of exile and the soft touch of love.

Not always satisfied with designs and shapes of which he was happily at liberty to draw, Chopin wished also to contain his thought within classical limits. He wrote beautiful *Concertos* and *Sonatas,* but in these productions it is not difficult to perceive more determination than inspiration. When inspired, he was demanding, uncontrolled, and impulsive. His actions could only be free, and we believe that he abused his genius whenever he sought to

35

subject it to rules, schemes, and forms that were foreign to him, that could not meet the dictates of his mind, one of those minds whose grace is specially displayed when seeming to work unfettered.

He was perhaps led to desire this double success by the example of his friend Mickiewicz. After being the first to endow his tongue with a fanciful poesy and, as early as 1818, founding a school in Slavic literature with his *Dziady* and romantic ballads, the latter then proved, by writing *Grazyna* and *Wallenrod*, that he could also conquer the difficulties that the burdens of classical form oppose to inspiration, that he was likewise master when he seized the lyre of ancient poets. In our opinion Chopin, in making similar attempts, was not so completely successful. He was not able to sustain, within the angular, unyielding squareness, that floating, indeterminate line that forms the charm of his thought. He was unable to force into it that hazy and blurred vagueness which rubs out its sharp edges and clothes it in long folds of fleecy mist such as surrounded Ossian's beauties as they conjured up for mortals some gentle outline in the midst of shifting clouds.

These attempts glow, however, through a rare distinction of style and embrace passages of high interest, sections of surprising grandeur. We shall mention the *Adagio* of the second *Concerto*, for which he had a marked fondness and which he frequently liked to repeat. The decorative designs belong to the author's finest manner, and the principal phrase shows an admirable breadth. It alternates with a recitative in the minor mode which serves as its foil. The whole piece is of an ideal perfection, its feeling radiant and compassionate by turn. It brings to mind a magnificent, light-bathed landscape, a blessed vale of Tempe, appropriate to a woeful tale or a melancholy scene, perhaps a hopeless misfortune enfolding the human heart amidst nature's matchless splendor—with contrast maintained by a fusion of tones and a softened diminution of hues [*une dégradation de teintes atténéries*[1]] that prevent any harshness or roughness from disturbing the moving impression thus produced. At the same time joy is tempered and sorrow is sweetened.

Could we fail to mention the *Marche funèbre* inserted in his first sonata, which was orchestrated and first performed at his burial service? Could any other accents have been found to express, with equal anguish, the feelings and tears that had to escort him to his final rest, him who so sublimely understood how great losses are mourned! One day we heard a young compatriot of his say: "Those pages could only have been written by a Pole!" And indeed, the full solemnity and heart-rending grief of a nation, weeping for its own death, is found in this funeral knell seemingly heading the mournful march. The very essence of mystical hope, of a holy call to super-human mercy, to infinite forbearance, and to justice that embraces every tomb and cradle—the entirety of exalted resignation, which has illumined with aureoles so many

1. *Sic.* This peculiar word was retained in subsequent editions. Probably *atténuées* was meant.—*Trans.*

sorrows and disasters borne with the heroism of Christian martyrs—these sound forth in the song of grieving supplication. Indescribably vibrant, it resounds and quickens and throbs with all that is most pure, most holy, most believing and most hoping in the hearts of women and children and priests. There is no impression here that a lone hero's death is bewept, since other heroes remain to avenge him; it is, rather, the death of a whole generation which, having vanished, leaves behind it only the women and children and priests. And yet this chant, so funereal and doleful, is possessed of such sweetness that it seems to be not of this world. These sounds, seemingly cool and distant, implant a profound contemplation as if they were sung by the very angels and were already floating in the heavens around the divine throne. No cries, no rough groans, no impious blasphemies, no raging imprecations disturb for a moment the lament, which could be likened to seraphic sighs. The ancient face of grief is totally shut out. Nothing recalls Cassandra's fury, Priam's abasement, Hecuba's frenzy, or the despair of the Trojan captives. The survivors of this Christian Ilium had a superb faith that swept away the bitterness of suffering as well as the cowardice of despair. No more does their grief hold aught of earthly weakness. It wrenches free from this land, damp with blood and tears, to fly toward God. It can only approach the supreme Judge with such poignant supplications that our hearts, hearing them, break beneath august compassion.

But it would be wrong to believe that all of Chopin's

compositions lack the feelings that he suppresses in this sublime outpouring, expression of energetic sacrifice and brave gentleness that cannot perhaps be long maintained. Muffled anger and stifled rage are met in many passages of his works, and several of his *Études*, his *Scherzos* likewise, paint a concentrated exasperation dominated by a despair that is now ironic and again haughty. These dark apostrophes of his muse have passed less noticed and less understood than his poems of a softer hue, and Chopin's personal character has contributed thereto. Kindly, gracious, easygoing, even-tempered, and animated, he gave slight cause to suspect the secret convulsions that shook him.

His character was not easy to grasp. It was composed of a thousand shades that, *a prima vista,* crossed and concealed each other in a mystifying way. It was easy to misjudge the depth of his thought, as is generally the case with Slavs whose honesty and openness, familiarity and charming *desinvoltura* of manners by no means imply confidence and effusion. Their feelings are revealed and hidden, like the twisted folds of a serpent entwined upon itself. (They must be carefully examined to discover the linkage of the rings.) It would be naïve to take literally their obsequious politeness or their outward modesty. The patterns of this politeness and modesty derive from their customs that strangely spring from their former relations with the Orient. Wholly free of Moslem taciturnity, they have learned from it a wary reserve on everything pertaining to sensitive and intimate matters—so much so that when they speak of themselves it is almost always certain that they exercise a reticence toward their questioner, thus assuring a mental or emotional advantage. The questioner remains ignorant of some circumstance or some secret motive through which they might be the more admired or the less esteemed, and which they hide behind a subtle, querying smile and an imperceptible scoffing. Ever delighting in the pleasure of mystification, from the wittiest and funniest to the most bitter and most ominous, they find in this mocking deceit, as it were, a pattern of scorn for the superiority which they inwardly assume, but which they veil with the care and guile of oppressed people.

Chopin's weak and sickly constitution prevented the vigorous expression of his passions, which he revealed to his friends only as gentle and affectionate. In the bustling, preoccupied world of great cities, where no one has leisure to guess the riddle of another's destiny, where each is judged only by his outward activity, surely very few think it worth while to explore beneath the surface of personal traits. But those who came close to Chopin in intimate and frequent relations had occasion to notice, sometimes, the impatience and vexation he felt at so promptly being taken literally. And the artist could not avenge the man! Too feeble in health to betray this impatience through the vehemence of his own playing, he sought compensation by writing pages that he loved to hear performed with the vigor that he lacked, pages in which swirl the passionate rancors of the man who is more grievously wounded than he is wont to admit. Similarly, around a flag-bedecked frigate, though about to founder, would swirl the fragments that the waves have torn from its sides.

These impressions have been all the more important in Chopin's life because they have obviously manifested themselves in his work. Little by little they attained a kind of unhealthy irascibility which, reaching the point of feverish agitation, produced that distortion, that twisting of thought, found in his final writings. Well-nigh suffocating, weighted down by his repressed violence, now using art only to tell himself his own tragedy after having sung his song, he began to subtilize it. In the leaves published under these influences is found something of the over-refined emotions of Jean Paul, who needed surprises springing from natural and physical phenomena, sensations of voluptuous terror born of happenings unforeseen in the natural order of things, morbid excitements of a brain bereft of reason in order to move a heart tormented by passions and indifferent to suffering. The melody becomes tortured, a nervous and restless sensibility brings about a rehandling of motives with a desperate persistence as painful as the agony of watching the ills of soul and body where death is the only relief. Chopin was prey to one of those ailments which, worsening from year to year, snatched him away still young—and in the productions whereof we speak there are to be found traces of the piercing pains that devoured him, just as would be found in a beautiful body the claw marks of a bird of prey.

2

THE POLONAISES AND
THEIR SOCIAL BACKGROUND

*T*HOSE ECCENTRICITIES OF FEELING, which however never lessen the rare quality of the harmonic fabric—on the contrary they make it more interesting to study—are seldom encountered in Chopin's best-known and most generally enjoyed pieces. His *Polonaises*, which are less familiar than they deserve to be because of the difficulties in their perfect performance, belong to his happiest inspirations. They do not in the slightest recall the mincing, made-up *Polonaises à la Pompadour* such as are heard from ballroom orchestras, from concert virtuosos, and in the hackneyed, faded repertoire of insipid, mannered, salon music. Energetic in rhythm, they completely startle and galvanize us from the torpor of indifference. The noblest traditional feelings of ancient Poland are embedded in them. An expression of firm determination joined to soberness—the hallmark, so to speak, of her great men of the past—is immediately noticeable. Largely martial in nature, they portray bravery and valor with the straightforwardness that was the distinctive trait of this warlike nation. They exude a calm, reflective strength and call to mind those ancient Poles as they are depicted in their chronicles: massive in frame, nimble in wit, deeply devout, invincibly brave, and possessed of a courtliness and gallantry which do not forsake the children of Poland on the field of battle, on the eve of combat, or on the day after. This courtliness was so inherent in their nature that—notwithstanding the restraint once imposed upon the women (derived from the customs of their neighbors and enemies, the infidels of Stamboul), confining them to domestic life and holding them in the shadow of legal wardship—in the course of history it led them to glorify and immortalize queens who became saints and vassals who became queens and beautiful subjects for whom some men risked and others lost thrones, as well as a terrible Sforza, an intriguing d'Arquien, and a coquettish Gonzaga.

With the Poles of olden times the blend of manly firmness with burning devotion to their loved ones (Sobieski, confronted by the banners of the Crescent *as thick as grain in a field,* was thus daily persuaded to send his wife tender love notes) assumed a strange, compulsive sway over their usual bearing, noble to the verge of pompousness. They could not fail to acquire a taste for all this as they observed the finest types of solemn ceremony among the followers of Islam whose qualities they appreciated and appropriated while combating their invasions. Like them they could preface their acts with an intelligent deliberateness that seemed to vitalize for each the motto of Prince Boleslas of Pomerania: *Erst wieg's, dann wag's,* "first weigh, then dare," and that set off their movements with a certain stately pride. It gave them an ease and freedom of spirit that was sensitive to the slightest show of tenderness, to the most fleeting fears of heart, to the most trifling affairs of life. As they staked their honor on charging dearly for life, they loved to adorn it and, even better, could love what did adorn it and revere what made it precious.

Their chivalric dignity was supported by their haughty manner, and since a firm premeditation added the fount of reason to the strength of valor, they succeeded in winning the admiration of all ages and of all minds, even of their very enemies. Here was a kind of reckless wisdom, of daring caution, of fatalistic fanaticism. Historically its most famous and outstanding manifestation was the expedition of Sobieski when he saved Vienna and struck a mortal blow against the Ottoman empire, conquered at last in that long struggle maintained by both sides with so much prowess, brilliance, and mutual respect between two enemies as irreconcilable in their clashes as they were magnanimous in their truces.

In listening to some of Chopin's *Polonaises* the imagination hears the heavy even more than determined tread of men, boldly valiant, who brave all that fate can offer of injustice. At times the imagination views the passage of magnificent groups such as Paul Veronese depicted, and the mind clothes them in the rich costume of past centuries: golden brocades, velvets, flowered satins, soft and flowing sables, sleeves casually tossed over the shoulder, inlaid sabers, rich jewels, boots red with trampled blood or golden yellow, sashes with sinuous fringes—restraining tuckers, pearl-encrusted bodices, rustling trains, headdresses sparkling with rubies or verdant with emeralds, slippers embroidered with amber, gloves perfumed with the scents of a harem. These groups stand out against the dim background of vanished time, surrounded by sumptuous Persian rugs, by filigreed furniture from Constantinople, by all the ostentatious lavishness of those grandees who, with their crimson goblets embossed with medallions, drew upon the fountains of Tokay. They shod their Arabian steeds with silver and topped their escutcheons with the same crown which, through election, might become royal and which, leading them to scorn any other title, was worn alone as badge of their glorious equality.

According to those who saw the Polish dance performed even as late as the opening of this century, it has degenerated so much that it is now difficult to grasp its original character. How lifeless it has become for them is readily understood upon reflection that most of the national dances are barely able to preserve their initial originality since the costume appropriate to it is no longer in use, and the Polonaise particularly is completely stripped of rapid movements and *steps* (that were truly choreographic) and unvarying, difficult poses. The Polonaise, devised far more for show than for seduction, was quickly

forced to drop its pompous importance and proud suffi-
ciency. It became a circulating promenade of slight interest
when men were deprived of the accessories essential, for
gestures in play and pantomime, in animating its pattern,
so simple but today decidedly dull. The many episodes and
the expressive miming that used to be introduced there
would be unimaginable were it not for the tales and examples of a few elders who still wear the ancient Polish
dress. By a rather rare exception this dance was destined to
emphasize men especially, to underline admiringly their
handsomeness, their fine bearing, and their martial and
courtly mien. (Do not these two epithets define the Polish
character?) In the original form the very name of the
dance is of masculine gender, and only through an obvious
misunderstanding was it transferred to the feminine.

Those who have never worn the *kontusz* of former
times (a kind of Occidental kaftan, the Oriental robe modified by the demands of an active life rarely yielding to
fatalistic resignation; a kind of *Férédgi*, often trimmed with
fur, which required frequent gestures capable of grace
and coquetry as the sleeves were tossed backward) would
find it difficult to appreciate the carriage, the slow bend-
ing, the sudden straightening, the subtleties of silent
pantomime which the ancients practiced as they filed past
in a Polonaise as in a military parade. Their fingers,
never left idle, played with their long mustaches or with
the handles of their swords. These were an integral part
of their costumes and constituted an object of vanity
regardless of age. Diamonds and sapphires often sparkled

on the weapon hung from belts of cashmere or of silk embroidered with gold and silver, setting off figures which were almost always somewhat corpulent. Even more often the mustache veiled, without concealing, some scar, which had a greater effect than the most precious stones. Since the luxury of materials and jewels and bright colors was as prevalent with the men as with the women, these stones were found (as in the Hungarian costume)[1] in buttons, in the inevitable rings, in neck-clasps, and in the aigrettes on brilliant velvet caps. During the Polonaise the ability to doff, to don, and to manipulate this cap easily and with the meaning attributed to these movements was an art in itself, chiefly noticeable in the knight of the leading couple who, as head of the line, gave the word of command to the whole company.

The master of the house opened each ball with this dance, not with the most beautiful or the most youthful, but with the most honored of the women present. Youth alone was not called to form the procession whose evolutions initiated every festival as if to offer a happy review as the first pleasure. After the master of the house, the most eminent persons came next. Choosing partners out of friendship or discretion, selecting their preferences or the most influential, they followed the steps of the leader. He had to perform a task less easy than today. He had to guide

1. In England the Hungarian costume worn by Prince Nicholas Esterházy at the coronation of George IV and valued at several million florins is still remembered.

47

the band organized in his charge in a thousand capricious meanderings through all the apartments where thronged the remaining guests. They would join the brilliant cortege later. They appreciated his reaching the most distant galleries, the garden plots, and the shrubbery where the music was heard only as a faint echo; but as if in revenge it welcomed the return to the main hall with a redoubling of fanfares. Arranged in hedgelike rows as he passed, the onlookers, constantly changing, watched him carefully. Never would he fail to lend his bearing and presence that dignity tempered with gaiety which won admiration from the women and jealousy from the men. Both vain and joyous, he would have believed himself lacking to his guests if he did not display, with a certain naïve piquancy, the pride he felt in seeing assembled in his home such illustrious friends and such notable followers, the chief concern of their visit being to array themselves richly to render him honor.

Guided by the host in this first rotation, the dancers encountered sudden turnings the effects of which came sometimes from surprises contrived in advance, sometimes from tricks of architecture or of decoration with embellishments in keeping with the pleasures of the day. The host would display them with pride or with some tribute *to the most valiant and the most beautiful* if they offered some topical allusion. The more these short excursions provided of the unexpected, and the more imaginative they were in amusing and happy invention, so the more the younger members of the company applauded, the more noisy were the acclamations, and the more joyous the peals of lovely laughter reaching the ears of the leader. Thus would he gain in reputation, becoming a privileged Coryphaeus and a much-sought-after partner. If he were already of a certain age, he would frequently receive, upon returning from one of these exploring rounds, deputations of girls coming to thank him and to compliment him in the name of all. Through their tales the pretty wanderers nourished the curiosity of guests and increased the zest with which later Polonaises were formed—for those who failed to be in this procession quietly watched its passage as if it were a shining comet.

For the persons assembled in the galleries—and in this land of aristocratic democracy it was no less important to astonish them, since they included many dependents of the great seigneurial houses, all noble (sometimes even more noble than the masters) but too poor to join in the festivities from which, moreover, they voluntarily abstained— this sumptuously elegant band, shedding iridescent hues and like a long serpent with shimmering rings, would first unreel its full length, then coil up again so that its sinuous contours in scintillant play would give the most varied nuances. Like muffled bells would come the sounds of golden chains, of heavy and magnificent damasks, of trailing sabers. Like a merry hiss the murmur of voices was heard from afar or, as it drew near, like the splashing waves of a flashing stream.

But the genius of hospitality, which in Poland seemed to spring as much from the refinements of civilization as from the touching simplicity of primitive manners—wanting in none of their innate courtesies—how could it be omitted from the details of their dance *par excellence?* After the master of the house had paid homage to his guests in opening the festival, each of them was entitled to claim his lady and replace him. Clapping his hands in order to halt the procession for a moment, the guest would bow before her as he begged for acceptance, while he who surrendered her would do the same with the couple next in line. This example was followed by all. The women, changing their cavaliers as often as a newcomer demanded the honor of leading the first among them, remained of course in unvarying order; but with the men, constantly replacing each other, it would happen that he who had begun the dance found himself to be the last, if not totally excluded before its close.

The cavalier who assumed the head of the column endeavored to excel his predecessor in skill through unusual combinations and through the patterns he made the line describe. Limited to a single room, these could attract attention by laying out graceful arabesques and even formal figures! He disclosed his art and his rights to the rôle he had seized by imagining figures that were tight-knit, complicated, and inextricable, by executing them nevertheless with such precision and assurance that the living ribbon, twisted in every direction, never broke apart in crossing its knots and never ended up in confusion or collision. The women and their partners, who only had to maintain the gait already set, were not allowed to follow idly over the floor. The step was rhythmic, measured, and undulating; it gave a harmonious swing to the entire body. There was no hasty rushing, no sudden shifting caused by impulsive motion. The dancers glided like swans descending a river, the imperceptible waves lifting and lowering their supple forms. The man would offer his lady now one hand, now the other, sometimes scarcely grazing the tips of her fingers, again enclosing them all within his palm. Never leaving her, he would circle to her left or to her right, and as each couple followed suit, these movements rippled through the whole extent of the gigantic serpent. Although preoccupied and apparently absorbed by these multiple maneuvers, the cavalier still found time to bend to his lady and profit from moments favorable for murmuring in her ear—sweet words if she was young, confidences, entreaties, and interesting tidbits if she was no longer so. Then, righting himself proudly, he would clang the steel of his weapons, twirl his mustache, and become so expressive in gesture that the woman had to yield an understanding response.

So it was no trite and meaningless promenade that was performed. It was, rather, if we may venture the thought, a procession wherein the entire company displayed its finery and self-admiringly preened itself on being so beautiful, so noble, so sumptuous, and so courtly. There was ceaseless show of its luster, its glories, its claims to fame. The men grown gray in campaigns and flights of oratory, captains more accustomed to wearing breastplates than robes of peace, high prelates and churchmen, great dignitaries of state, elderly senators, warlike palatines, and ambitious castellans—these were the dancers awaited, desired, and disputed by the youngest, gayest, and most brilliant ladies who were involved in transient choices. Honor and honors equalized the years and could gain an advantage over love itself. Upon being told by those who had not wished to abandon the ancient *zupan* and *kontusz* (with head close-shaven around the temples like their ancestors) of the forgotten evolutions and the vanished felicities of this majestic dance, we understood the depth of this proud nation's embedded instinct for display. We understood its need therefor and, through the quality of graciousness inherited from nature, how much it poeticized this taste for ostentation by commingling the reflection of noble feelings and the charm of high resolves.

When we found ourselves in the country of Chopin, his memory with us like a guide whetting the curiosity, we fortunately encountered several of those individuals who, day by day in every place, are becoming more rare. Such is the effect of European civilization which, though it does not change the essence of national characteristics, at least erases and refines their roughness and outward form. Some of these men that we had the good fortune to encounter were of a superior intelligence, cultivated, erudite, and mightily developed through a life of action, but their horizon was limited by the boundaries of their land, their society, their literature, and their traditions. In our talks with them (made possible or facilitated by an interpreter), in their manner of judging the substance and forms of new customs, we could catch glimpses of the past and of what contributed to their greatness, their charm, and their weakness. That originality, inimitable when narrowly considered, is curious to observe. By lessening the value of opinions on many matters, it nevertheless endows the mind with a peculiar strength, with a sharp and primitive perceptivity relating to cherished interests, and with an energy that nothing can mitigate. Everything beyond its purpose is foreign to it, and alone it can portray, like a faithful mirror, the panorama of the past, preserving its color, true light, and picturesque setting. It, and it only, reflects at the same time the ritual of disappearing customs and the spirit that created them.

Chopin had come too late and left home too early to possess this quality. But he had known numerous examples, and through the memories surrounding his childhood, surely better than through his country's history and poetry, he found by induction the secret of its ancient glories, which he retrieved from neglect and, in his songs, endowed with eternal youth. And as every poet is better understood, better appreciated by travelers who, seeking the source of their visions, have visited the places that inspired him—as Pindar and Ossian are more intimately revealed to those who view the remains of the Parthenon radiant in atmospheric brightness and the mist-veiled beauties of Scotland —similarly Chopin's fount of inspiration is disclosed fully only to those who have been in his land. They have seen there the shadow left by passing centuries, have followed its swelling embrace that enwraps like night, and have encountered that phantom of glory, restless spirit, that permeates his heritage. Frightening and burdening all hearts, it appears when least expected. It shows itself in the tales and recollections of olden times. It brings a terror like unto that diffused among the peasants of the Ukraine by the beautiful virgin who is pale as Death and is ceintured with a crimson sash. She appears, they say, to mark with a spot of blood the gates of villages destined for destruction.

Throughout long centuries Poland formed a state whose great civilization was wholly autochthonous, similar to no other and necessarily unique of its kind. As different from the feudal system of Germany, her western neighbor, as from the conquering spirit of the Turks, who persistently troubled her eastern boundaries, she nevertheless was drawn toward Europe by a knightly Christianity and an equal passion for fighting infidels. From the masters of Byzantium she received instruction in political sagacity, military tactics, and weighty discourse, fusing heterogeneous elements into a society that harbored the causes of ruin and decay along with the heroic qualities of Moslem fanaticism and the sublime virtues of Christian holiness.[2] The general cultivation of Latin learning, knowledge of and taste for Italian and French literature, shed upon these strange contrasts a luster and a sheen of classicism. It was

2. The number of glorious names with which Poland has enriched the calendar and martyrology of the Church is well known. The court of Rome granted to the order of the Trinitarians, or the *Redemptorist Brothers*, destined to redeem Christians enslaved by infidels, the exclusive privilege of wearing a red ceinture on a white habit. This was in memory of the Order's many martyrs, chiefly from establishments close to the frontier, such as the one in Kamieniec-Podolski.

inevitable that this civilization, even in its last manifestations, should assume a distinctive character. Little favoring tales of knight-errantry or tournaments of jousting exhibitions, as was natural for a nation constantly at war, and reserving its deeds of valor for the enemy, Poland substituted for tourney games and splendors fêtes of a different kind in which magnificent processions were the principal features.

There is surely no novelty in asserting that a whole aspect of a people's character is disclosed in their national dances. But we believe there are few in which, marked by such a grand simplicity of motion as in the Polonaise, the life-giving impulses are conveyed so perfectly in their totality and are revealed so variedly in the episodes that were inserted individually into the general plan. As soon as these episodes had disappeared, when their zestfulness was gone, when a rôle for these short interludes could no longer be imagined, when satisfaction resulted from the mechanical traversing of a salon, then only the skeleton of ancient ceremony remained.

We should certainly have hesitated to speak of the Polonaise after the beautiful verses devoted to it by Mickiewicz and the admirable description that he inserted in the final canto of *Pan Tadeusz* if it were not part of a work as yet untranslated and known only to the poet's compatriots. Even under another form it would have been rash to approach a subject already sketched and colored by such a brush in that familiar, epic romance. Its beauties, of the highest order, are enframed in a scene such as Ruysdaël would paint in directing a ray of sunlight between two storm clouds onto one of those trees rarely lacking from his canvas, onto a birch shattered by lightning, its gaping wound seeming to redden the white bark with blood. The action of *Pan Tadeusz* occurs at the beginning of our century, when there were still many who represented the feelings and solemn manners peculiar to the ancient Poles. There were others, too, already swayed by the graceful, giddying passions of modern origin: types that were then contrasting and striking, and to be quickly effaced by the conventionalism that invades and molds the elite society of all capitals and all countries. Chopin was certainly inspired many times by this poem, its scenes lending so much to the painting of emotions that he loved to reproduce.

No examples of Polonaises more than a century old have been preserved, and their primitive music has little artistic value. Some, bearing no composer's name, are occasionally associated with heroes, and their date is thus indicated. For the most part they are serious and gentle. The *Polonaise* called *de Kosciuszko* is the most widely known. It is so firmly linked to the memory of its period that we have seen women, recollecting as they listened, unable to hear it without bursting into sobs. In her last days, when age had weakened all her faculties, the Princess F— L—, once beloved of Kosciuszko, was responsive only to those chords that her trembling hands still drew from the keyboard, her eyes no longer seeing the keys. Some other contemporaneous pieces in this style are of so plaintive a character that, on first hearing, they would be taken for the notes of a funeral train.

The *Polonaises* of Count Ogiński,[3] coming next, soon attained a great popularity by their blend of languor with a doleful mood. Still affected by that darkening color, they alter it by a tenderness of sad and naïve charm. Rhythm subsides, transition sets in, as if the procession, once solemn and forceful, were becoming silent and rapt as it passes near the graves where pride and laughter are stifled. Wandering in these surroundings only love survives, repeating the refrain that the bard of *green Erin* snatched from the breezes of his isle: *"Love born of sorrow, like sorrow, is true!"* (*L'amour de la douleur est vrai comme elle*).

In Ogiński's well-known pages there can always be imagined a distich of similar thought borne on two loving sighs or revealed in eyes that are moist with tears.

Later the tombs are gone—they retreat, and are seen only distantly. Life and animation reappear. Mournful impressions change into memories and return only as echoes. No more does the imagination evoke the shades that glide warily lest they awaken the dead of yesterday—and already in the *Polonaises* of Lipiński the heart is heard, joyous and carefree, beating as it did before disaster. The melody is drawn more clearly and exudes a perfume of youth and springtime love. It flows into an expressive, sometimes dreamlike song; it speaks only to youthful hearts, wafting

3. One, in F major, has remained especially famous. It was published with a vignette showing the author blowing out his brains with a pistol, a romantic commentary that was long, though wrongly, accepted as fact.

(This composer was probably Prince Michael Cleophas Ogiński [1765–1833], diplomat, author, and musician. His polonaises, more emotional than earlier specimens, were widely known in Europe.—*Trans.*

to them poetic fancies. Its purpose is not to measure the tread of exalted and solemn figures who now have little share in the dances for which it was written.[4] It appeals to romantic and vibrant imaginations more concerned with pleasures than splendors. Meyseder [sic] proceeded down this path and achieved the sprightliest coquetry and the most charming over-all liveliness. His imitators have submerged us in compositions entitled *Polonaise,* but they no longer have any character justifying the name.[5]

With one stroke a man of genius restored its vigorous brilliance. Weber[6] turned the Polonaise into a dithyramb wherein all the vanished magnificence and its dazzling deployment were suddenly rediscovered. To echo the past in a formula become diluted, he brought together the varied resources of his art. Without seeking to recall the nature of ancient music, he infused into it the very essence of the ancient Polonaise. He emphasized rhythm. He dramatized the melody, coloring it through modulation with a lavishness that the subject not only suggested but

4. Primates and bishops formerly participated in these dances, but in recent times the ecclesiastical personnel withdrew.

5. Karol Lipiński (1790–1861) and Joseph Mayseder (1789–1863), respectively Polish and Austrian violinists and composers, whose polonaises were well known.—*Trans.*

6. Carl Maria von Weber (1786–1826), in addition to making major contributions to opera, was an important composer of piano music. Liszt was well acquainted with his *Grande Polonaise,* Op. 21, and his *Polacca brillante,* Op. 72, composed respectively in 1808 and 1819. In making his celebrated version of Weber's "Polonaise brillante" for piano and orchestra, Liszt prefixed the slow introduction of the earlier work to the scintillant body of the latter.—*Trans.*

absolutely demanded. He injected into the Polonaise life and warmth and passion, without ignoring the haughty air, the formally pompous dignity, the majesty both natural and affected that are its inherent characteristics. The cadences were marked by chords calling to mind the sound of sabers shaken in their scabbards. The murmur of voices, instead of relaying pallid twitterings of love, resounded with bass tones, full and deep, like those accustomed to command. Such voices attract the fiery, distant neighing of those desert steeds, so nobly and elegantly built, that fretfully paw the ground and gaze with gentle, intelligent and flashing eye—and carry so gracefully the long trappings, trimmed with turquoises or rubies, which the Polish lords would pile upon them.[7] Did Weber know the Poland of old? Had he evoked a picture already contemplated in order thus to establish the association? Idle questions!

7. At the time of its splendor the treasury of the Princes Radziwill in the district of Nieswirz contained twelve harnesses inlaid with precious stones, each of a different color. There, too, were the twelve apostles, life-size, in solid silver. This luxury is by no means astonishing in the reflection that this family, descended from the last grand pontiff of Lithuania (who, upon embracing Christianity, was given outright all the woods and lands previously consecrated to the cult of pagan deities), still owned 800,000 serfs toward the end of the last century, although its wealth had diminished considerably. A no less curious item in this treasure, and still existing, is a picture of St. John the Baptist draped in a shoulder-sash bearing this legend: *In the name of the Lord, John, thou shalt be conqueror.* It was found by *John* Sobieski himself, after the victory he won under the walls of Vienna, in the tent of the Grand Vizir Kara-Mustapha. Following his death, Marie d'Arquin gave it to a Prince Radziwill, with an inscription in her own hand indicating its origin and her donation. The autograph and the royal seal are on the back of the canvas.

Does not Genius have its intuitions, and does Poetry ever fail to reveal to Genius what lies in its domain?

In approaching his subjects Weber showed an ardent and tense imagination which drew from them, like sap, their full content of poetry and gained so absolute a mastery that it was difficult to follow him with any hope of achieving the same effects. Chopin, however, surpassed him in this inspired vein, both by the quantity and variety of writings in this *genre* and by his more moving style and new harmonic procedures. His *Polonaises* in A and A flat major especially resemble Weber's in E major in shape and temperament. In others he relinquished this breadth of manner. He treated this idea differently, but shall we say still more happily? In matters of this sort judgment is a thorny thing. How are the rights of the poet over varied phases of his subject to be restrained? Should he not be allowed to be dark and oppressed in the midst of joy, to sing of grief after having chanted of glory, to lament with those who mourn after repeating the shouts of those who prosper? Surely not the least of Chopin's superiorities lay in successively exploiting all of this theme's possibilities, in exhausting its full measure of brilliance with its full measure of sadness. The phases of his emotions resulted in a multiplicity of views. Their transformations and their frequent suffering can be followed in the series of these particular works, and the fertility of his spirit demands admiration even when it is no longer sustained and prolonged by freshness of inspiration. He did not always limit himself to the group of pictures supplied by his memory and imagination. More than once, in viewing parts of the brilliant crowd passing before him, he became enamored of some isolated face, was caught by the magic of its glance. He delighted in musing on its mysterious revelations and sang thenceforth for it alone.

The *Grand Polonaise in F sharp minor* must be ranked among his strongest conceptions. Interpolated therein is a *Mazurka*, a novelty that might have become an ingenious ballroom caprice had he not frightened frivolousness away with a darkening humor in a fantastic evocation. It could be likened to the first glimmer of a winter dawn, dull and gray, the tale of a dream after a sleepless night, a dream-poem where impressions and objects unfold with strange incoherencies and strange transitions, like those described by Byron in his poem entitled A *Dream:*

. . . Dreams in their development have breath,
And tears, and tortures, and the touch of Joy;
They have [leave] a weight upon our waking thoughts, . . .
And look like heralds of Eternity.

The principal motive has an ominous air, like the hour before the hurricane; desperate exclamations seem to fall upon the ear, a defiance hurled at all the elements. And forthwith the insistent reappearance of a tonic at the beginning of each measure brings to mind the repeated firing of a cannon in a distant, hard-fought battle. Following this note, measure by measure, appear strange harmonies. Even in the greatest authors we know nothing analogous to the striking effect of this section, which is abruptly interrupted by a pastoral scene, by an idyllic *Mazurka* seeming to issue

scents of lavender and sweet marjoram. But far from eras-
ing the memory of the deep and unhappy feeling that first
prevailed, it increases on the contrary, through ironic and
bitter contrast, the painful emotions of the listener—to
such a point that he well-nigh experiences relief when the
first phrase returns and he views again the depressing, imposing spectacle of a fatal struggle, freed at least from the
persistent opposition of a mean and naïve happiness! This
improvisation ends like a dream, with no other conclusion
than a dismal shudder that leaves the soul in the grip of a
single, dominant impression.

In the *Polonaise-Fantaisie*, already belonging to the
last period of Chopin's works, to those which are over-
shadowed by a feverish apprehension, there is no trace of
bold and shining pictures. There is no sound of the joyous
tramp of cavalry accustomed to victory, of songs which
no foretaste of defeat can silence, of words coming from
the daring spirit suited to conquerors. An elegiac sadness reigns here, broken by startled movements, melancholy smiles, and sudden gasps. There is a restless calm
such as is felt by people surprised in ambush and who,
surrounded on all sides, see no hope along the vast horizon.
Despair mounts in their brain like a copious draft of that
Cyprus wine which gives a more instinctive speed to all
gestures, a sharper point to all words, a more scorching
spark to all emotions, and then brings the mind to a pitch
of irritability bordering on delirium.

Paintings of slight value to art, like those of all last
moments, of death pangs and moans, of spasms with mus-

cles losing all flexibility and nerves no longer the organs of will—so is man doomed to become no more than the passive prey of woe! Pitiable manifestations that the artist can usefully incorporate in his work only with extreme caution!

3

THE MAZURKAS AND
THEIR SOCIAL BACKGROUND

*A*s far as expression is concerned, Chopin's *Mazurkas* are notably different from his *Polonaises*. Their character is totally dissimilar. They constitute another world wherein delicate, nebulous, and shifting nuances replace a color that is rich and strong. The single, indivisible soul of a whole people yields to purely personal, constantly individualized impressions. Instead of being thrust into a somewhat hazy background the feminine (and effeminate) element becomes clearly conspicuous, attaining a position of such prominence indeed that other elements vanish before it or, at least, only serve as its accompaniment. No longer do the times permit calling a woman *grateful* [*reconnaissante, wdzięczna*] if she was charming, the very word for charm deriving from *gratitude* [*wdzięki*]. Woman no longer appears as a favored one, but as a queen; she no longer seems to be the best part of life—she is all of it. Man is hot-

64

headed, proud and arrogant, but he is drawn to the vortex
of pleasure. Yet this pleasure is ever streaked with melancholy, and the words and music (rarely separated) of national songs reflect the two extremes. Together they present
that contrast of strangely attractive effect, caused in reality
by the need to *gladden sorrow* [*ciezsyc bide*], which culmi-
nates in a bewildering delight in the mazurka with its
graces and furtive fancies. The words that are sung to the
melodies, moreover, grant the privilege of associating more
intimately with the life of recollection than other dance
tunes allow. Fresh and ringing voices have repeated them
many times, in solitude, in early morning hours, and in moments of cheerful leisure. Have they not been hummed on
a journey, in the woods, on a boat, when emotion suddenly
overwhelms or when an encounter, a scene, an unhoped-
for word flashes imperishably through the heart—hours
destined to shine in memory across the most distant years
and the farthest reaches of the future?

Chopin seized upon these inspirations most happily
and brought to them the full benefit of his technic and
style. Cutting them, like diamonds, into a thousand facets,
he exposed all their latent fire, and in their reassembly, even
to the particles of dust, he mounted them like streaming
jewels. In what other setting, indeed, could his personal
memories have assisted him better in creating poems, presenting scenes, describing events or unfolding tales which,
thanks to him, spread far beyond the soil that gave them
birth and now belong to those idealized types consecrated
by art in its shining, lustrous kingdom?

To understand how appropriate this setting was to the

shades of feeling that Chopin, with an iridescent hand, brought to it, it is essential to have seen the mazurka danced in Poland. Only thus can its pride and tenderness and piquancy be grasped. The man chosen by his partner proudly claims her like a conquest and presents her for his rivals' admiration before whisking her away in a whirling, voluptuous embrace that does not conceal the defiant expression of the victor and the blushing vanity of the prize, whose beauty makes the glory of his triumph. There are few more delightful scenes than a ball in that country when, the mazurka once begun, the attention of the entire room, far from obscured by a crowd of persons colliding from opposite directions, is drawn to a single couple, each of equal beauty, darting forth into empty space. The cavalier at first accentuates his steps as if hurling a challenge, parts from his companion for a moment as if to view her better, closes with her at once with passionate eagerness, or even turns full circle as if mad with joy and suddenly giddy. Sometimes two couples start out at the same time, and it happens that the men may change ladies, or that a third man appears, clapping his hands, to snatch a lady from her partner. Then the queens of the festival are claimed in turn by the most brilliant young men who court the honor of gaining their hand.

While the waltz and the galop isolate the dancers and offer the onlookers only a picture of confusion; while the quadrille can be likened to a passage at arms with foils, the attack and parry being done with an equal unconcern and casual grace that evoke only casual response; while the

vivaciousness of the polka, admittedly charming, easily becomes equivocal; while the fandangos, tarantellas, and
minuets are little love-dramas of various kinds which interest only the performers, the man's sole task being to
show off his lady as the public, rather grumpily, merely
follows the coquetries in their necessary but meaningless
pantomime—in the mazurka, on the contrary, the crowd
has a part to play, and the man's rôle is second to his partner's in neither importance nor grace.

The long intervals separating the successive appearance of couples are given over to the chatter of the dancers.
When their turn comes again, the scene no longer passes
among themselves, but between them and the assembled
throng. Before the latter, the man shows he is proud of
her whose favor he has been able to win; before it, too,
the lady pays honor to her partner, and she also seeks to
please the throng because its approbation, bestowed upon
her partner, becomes for him the most flattering blandish-
ment. At the last moment she seems to proffer this approval formally by darting toward him and resting on his
arm. It is a movement which, above all others, is capable
of a thousand nuances, from outbursts of passion to the
most aimless abandon, that are governed by feminine wile
and charm.

And what varied manifestations there are, too, in the
turns around the ballroom! Beginning at first with a kind
of shy hesitation, the lady tenses like a bird about to take
flight. A long glide on one foot alone and she skims like
a skater over the ice-smooth floor; she runs like a child and

suddenly bounds in the air. Like a goddess of the hunt, with eyes wide open, head erect, and bosom high, she sails in nimble leaps through the air like a boat riding the waves and seems to disport herself in space. Then she re-enters her dainty glide, surveys the spectators, directs a few smiles and words to the most favored, raises her lovely arms to the knight coming to rejoin her, and resumes the agile steps that carry her with amazing speed from one end of the hall to the other. She glides, she runs, she flies. Exertion colors her cheeks and brightens her glance, bows her figure and slows her pace until, panting and exhausted, she gently sinks and falls into the arms of her partner, who seizes her firmly and raises her for a moment into the air before they finish the intoxicating round.

The most diverse configurations vary and enliven this triumphal passage, which produces many an Atalanta as beautiful as Ovid ever dreamed of. In a leading chain all the couples first clasp hands. Forming a great circle that briefly whirls around with dazzling effect, they weave a crown wherein each woman is a flower unique of her kind, while the standard costume of the men, like dark foliage, sets off the shifting colors. They dash forth altogether, in sparkling verve and jealous competition, parading before the spectators like a review. Separately detailed they would be scarcely less interesting than the enumeration of armies by Homer and Tasso, ready for alignment in battle array. At the end of an hour or two the same circle re-forms to end the dance—and on the days when diversion and pleasure infect everyone with a wild gaiety, running through these impressionable beings like a crackling fire of dried vines, the general promenade is resumed once more. Its accelerated pace allows no suspicion of the slightest weariness in the delicate and persistent women whose limbs seem possessed of steel's responsive and untiring flexibility.

Instinctively all the women in Poland possess the magic knowledge of this dance. Even the least happily endowed can find there improvised allurements. It favors shyness and modesty as well as the stateliness of those who are aware that they are the most envied. Is this not so because, of all dances, it is the most chastely amorous? The dancers do not ignore the surrounding throng; on the contrary, they address themselves to it—and in the very essence of the dance there reigns a mingling of intimate tenderness and mutual vanity as decorous as it is compelling.

Chopin released the poetic *unknown* which was only suggested in the original themes of Polish *Mazurkas*.[1] He preserved the rhythm, ennobled the melody, enlarged the proportions, and infused a harmonic chiaroscuro as novel as the subjects it supported—all this in order to paint in these productions (which he loved to hear us call *easel pictures*) the innumerable and so widely differing emotions that excite the heart while the dance goes on, especially in those long intervals when the cavalier, by right and steadfastly, holds a place beside his lady.

1. The mazurka is said to have originated in the region of Mazovia, which includes Warsaw. Examples can be traced back to the early sixteenth century.—*Trans.*

Flirtations, conceits, fancies, attachments, laments, passions developed and awakening, conquests on which may depend another's fate or favor—all are encountered in this dance. But how difficult it is to appreciate fully the infinite degrees of passion, halting or rising and kindled for longer or shorter periods with as much abandon as mischief, in those lands where the mazurka holds sway from the palace to the hut: in those lands where the qualities and faults peculiar to a nation are so oddly apportioned that, though almost essentially the same everywhere, they change and shift so surprisingly in their mingling that they often become unrecognizable! Consequently there is, in characteristics thus capriciously blended, an extreme diversity which uniquely spurs the curiosity, encourages a piquant investigation of each new relationship, and lends meaning to the slightest incidents. Here there is nothing banal, indifferent or unnoticed. Contrasts multiply in these natures which are forever restless in their impressions. They have an alert, keen, and subtle mind, and a sensitivity, nourished by misfortune and suffering, that unexpectedly illumines their hearts as the flames of fire dispel darkness. In these lands, moreover, chance can bring close together those who were strangers the night before. The ordeal of a minute or a murmur may divide hearts long united. Sudden confidences are forced, and hopeless mistrust is maintained in secret. According to the word of a witty woman: "One often plays comedy to escape tragedy." Constantly there is conveyed to the mind what must not be uttered. Generalities serve to sharpen, while concealing, interrogation, and they bring forth the most evasive responses, as sound is struck from an object to ascertain its metal. Pleading for others is a pretense for pleading for self, and flatteries may be only disguised exactions.

And then a stubborn attention that finally annoys expansive dispositions, a tiring levity—astonishing before its desperate indifference is disclosed—supplements, as if in irony, the most witty refinement and the actuality of the most fitting grief in their most poetic expression. But, real or apparent in turn, it eludes ready and easy understanding. Strange responses cause it to assume, wrongly as often as rightly, the aspect of a gaily colored veil, and a rip in the fabric would be enough to reveal more than one quality dormant or buried in its folds. Thus it happens that high-flown talk is often only solemn jesting flashing with sparks of wit like the play of fireworks, the warmth of speech being devoid of seriousness, while at other times carelessly uttered jokes are sadly sober. Untimely mirth follows close upon bitter and fierce introversion. Nothing remains wholly superficial, although neither does anything escape the polish of artificiality. And there where conversation is an art developed to the highest degree, demanding an enormous share of everyone's time, few of the joyful or sorrowful remarks that are heard relieve one of doubt as he listens to a person able to pass in a moment from laughter to grief, the sincerity of either being difficult to judge.

Like beds of quicksand on the shores of certain seas, the ideas in these shifting modes of thought are rarely recovered in their original form. This alone would suffice

71

to lend a special stamp to the most insignificant conversations, as we learned from a few men of that country who won the admiration of Parisian society for their marvelous ability to fence in paradox. It is a skill that every Pole possesses more or less, according to the degree of his interest or enjoyment in cultivating it. But the inimitable zest that impels him constantly to change the garb of truth and fiction, to display each always in the other's guise, like touchstones, all the more certain as they are the less suspect —that zest which, wildly lavish, expends a prodigious mental effort on the most trivial occasions (like Gil Blas using as much intelligence to find the means of living a single day as the King of Spain in ruling his domains)—that zest makes as breathless an impression as the games of the famed Indian jugglers who, with unheard-of skill, flash and toss through the air a quantity of sharp and cutting weapons which, at the slightest slip, would become instruments of death. It alternately hides and discloses anxiety, anguish, and fright whenever complicated positions suggest a danger in any carelessness, accident, or error, and a powerful assistance from some obscure and forgotten individual. A dramatic interest can then suddenly arise in the least important interviews and give to every relationship the least-suspected aspects. A misty uncertainty hovers over the slightest encounters. It never allows the fixing of lines or establishing of contours, of distinguishing present or future limits, and this makes them all complex, indefinable, and intangible. They are filled with a vague and hidden terror, a subtle flattery capable of self-renewal, and a sympathy often straining to be released from these pressures. These three qualities are entangled in the heart in a hopeless confusion of patriotic, vain, and amorous feeling.

And so—what emotions are clustered together in the accidental meetings brought about by the mazurka. The slightest whims of the heart are lent enchantment; the most distant, idle, and momentary encounters appeal to the imagination! And how could it be otherwise, in the presence of women who give to the mazurka that graciousness that other countries vainly endeavour to attain? For are not Slavic women beyond compare? There are some among them whose qualities and virtues are so absolute that they belong to all ages and to all lands, but these spirits are always and everywhere rare. Most of them are distinguished by a diverse originality. Half-Egyptian, half-Parisian, preserving from mother to daughter, perhaps, the secret of flaming philters consumed in harems, they attract by Asiatic languor, by the flashing of hourilike eyes, by the indolence of a sultana, by the revelation of inexpressible tenderness, by gestures that caress without encouraging, by motions that are wondrously deliberate, by a pliant grace that is flowingly magnetic. They attract by that lissomeness of figure which is unrestrained and never stiffened through ceremony, by those vocal intonations that startle and summon tears from unknown depths of the heart, by impulsive gestures that recall the spontaneity of a gazelle. They are, moreover, intelligent and informed, quick in comprehension, skilled in utilizing their knowledge, and strangely versed in the divination of character;

yet they are superstitious and avid, like the beautiful, ignorant creatures who worship the Arabian prophet. Generous and courageous, rapturous and nobly reverent, loving danger and loving love, from which they ask much and to which they give little, they especially adore glory and fame. Heroism delights them. Not one among them, perhaps, would fear paying too dearly for a dazzling deed. And yet it must be said, in solemn respect, that many of them, mysteriously sublime, practice their holiest virtues and finest sacrifices in obscurity. But however exemplary the merits of their home life, as long as their youth endures (and it is as long as it is premature), neither the vexations of intimate existence nor the hidden griefs that rend souls too passionate to escape frequent wounding suppress the marvelous vivacity of their emotions which they can impart with the infallibility of an electric spark. Naturally and socially discreet, they wield the great weapon of dissimulation with incredible skill. They probe the soul of others and keep their own secrets locked up. It is often the noblest that are concealed, with a haughtiness that shrinks from self-display. The inward scorn they have for those that do not fathom them affirms that superiority wherewith they so artfully reign over all the hearts they can bewitch or flatter, tame or capture—hearts which they dominate with all the ardor of their being, even to the point of confronting and sharing death, exile, prison, and the cruelest sufferings, ever faithful, ever compassionate, ever unswervingly devoted.

An irresistible composite, fascinating and honored,

that M. de Balzac has sketched in completely antithetical lines enclosing the most precious of incense offered to that "daughter of a foreign land who is an angel through love, a demon through fantasy, a child through faith, an elder through experience, a man in brain and a woman in heart, a giant through hope, a mother through sorrow, and a poet through her dreams."[2]

Polish women have always inspired fervent homage, for they all have a poetic comprehension of an ideal that they reflect in their remarks, like an image ever present in a mirror that they fancy can be caught. Despising the weak and too-facile pleasure of merely pleasing, they would have the pleasure of admiring those who love them. Romantic sustenance of their desires, it sometimes holds them in long hesitation between the world and the cloister where, at some moment of her life, nearly every one of them has earnestly and bitterly thought of seeking refuge.

There, where such beings reign supreme, what feverish words, what hopes and despair, what illusions and delightful rapture must have welled forth in the patterns of these *Mazurkas*, each one lingering in the mind of every Polish woman like the echo of a vanished passion or a soulful declaration? Who among them has not finished a mazurka with cheeks brighter from emotion than from weariness? What unexpected ties came from these long and throng-surrounded pairings, the strain of music usually recalling some warlike name, some historic memory suggested by the words and linked forever to the

2. Dedication of *Modeste Mignon* [to Mme Hanska].

melody? What vows were exchanged there, what hard farewells there uttered! What brief attachments have been joined and disjoined in one evening, between those who were strangers at meeting, who would come together no more, yet who could not forget the other! What painful emotions could only be disclosed in those single moments when beauty is more admired than wealth and graciousness more than rank! What destinies, sundered by wealth and rank, were able to cross only in these recurrent encounters, shining with triumph and hidden joy! What conversations, carelessly begun and extended in irony, interrupted with feeling and resumed in innuendo (where Slavic wit and subtlety excel) have led to deep affection! What confidences have been scattered there in the unfolding frankness of stranger to stranger, free of the tyranny of imposed conventions! What deceptively laughing words, what promises and desires and vague hopes were there cast casually to the wind, like the handkerchief of the lady in the mazurka—and which the clumsy failed to retrieve!

As we have said, perhaps it is essential to know well Chopin's feminine compatriots in order to sense the feelings that permeate his *Mazurkas* and many more of his compositions besides. Nearly all are filled with that same amorous mist that saturates his *Préludes, Nocturnes*, and *Impromptus* which evoke, one by one, all the expressions of passion: charming lures of coquetry; unwary surrender of inclinations; whimsical festoonings wrought of fantasy; fatal despondency of barren joys which are born a-dying;

flowers of mourning like those black roses of depressing fragrance, their petals dropping from fragile stems at the slightest breath; weakened flashes kindled by false vanities, similar to the shine of certain lifeless woods that glisten in darkness; pleasures without past or future snatched from chance encounters; illusions, unexplainable fancies that summon us to adventure like those tart flavors of half-ripened fruit that please while setting the teeth on edge; suggestions of emotion of endless range augmented by the vital poesy, innate nobility, beauty and distinction and elegance of those who feel them.

In most of Chopin's *Ballades*, *Valses*, and *Études*, as well as in the pieces just mentioned, there lies embalmed the memory of an elusive poesy, and this he sometimes idealizes to the point of presenting its essence so diaphanous and fragile that it seems no longer to be of our world. It brings closer the realm of fairies and unveils to us unguarded secrets of the Peri, of Titanias or Ariels or Queen Mabs, of all the genii of water, air, and fire, who are also the victims of the most bitter frustrations and the most intolerable aversions.

At times these pieces are joyous and fanciful, like the gambolings of an amorous, mischievous sylph. At other times they are velvety and multicolored, like the dress of a salamander. Then they are deeply depressing, like souls in torment who find no prayer of mercy needed for their salvation. Again, these pieces are stamped with a despair so dismal and inconsolable that they bring to mind a tragedy of Byron, the scene of Jacopo Foscari's ultimate downfall and failure to survive his exile. There are some with spasms of choking sobs. And there are also some that are witty and bantering wherein only the black keys of the piano are touched. They recall the gaiety of Chopin who, lover of the Attic spirit as he was, touched only the upper levels of the mind and retreated from vulgar humor, coarse laughter, and rough play as from animals, more disgusting than dangerous, whose sight causes the most nauseous repulsion in certain soft and sensitive natures.

An extreme variety of subjects and impressions prevails in the great quantity of his *Mazurkas*. Several are colored by the rattling of spurs, but in most of them and distinguishable above all else are the imperceptible rustling of crepe and gauze beneath the airy lightness of the dance, the murmur of fans, and the clinking of gold and diamonds. Some seem to paint the brave but fear-ridden pleasure of a ball on the eve of an assault. Sighs and faltering farewells are heard through the rhythm of the dance, which cloaks all tears. Others seem to bare the anguish, the pains and secret torments brought to parties where the uproar fails to stifle the outcries of the heart. In still others there is the effect of smothered terrors: fears, forebodings of a love that struggles and, devoured by jealousy, survives to feel its defeat, disdaining to curse and seeking shelter in pity. Elsewhere there is a whirlwind, a delirium, pierced by a gasping, broken melody like the throbbing of a heart that swoons and shatters and is dying of love. Elsewhere, too, resound faint fanfares, like glory's distant recollection. And there are some with rhythm as flexible and flowing as the emotion of two young lovers gazing at a solitary star high in the heavens!

One evening only three of us were together. Chopin had played for some time, and one of the most distinguished women of Paris felt more and more overcome by a solemn composure, such as arises from viewing the gravestones scattered over those fields in Turkey where shadows and flower plots, from afar, promise the astonished visitor a smiling garden. She asked him whence came the involuntary veneration that bowed her heart before monuments visible only as soft and gentle objects, and by what name he called the remarkable emotion poured into his compositions like ashes of the nameless in splendid urns of finest alabaster? Won by the lovely tears that dampened such lovely eyes and with a frankness rare in the artist sensitive to everything calling for intimate disclosures, which he buried in the brilliant mountings of his works, he replied: her heart had not deceived her in its melancholy gloom, for, regardless of his transient joys, he was never free of a feeling which somehow formed the base of his heart and for which the expression was found only in his own language, no other having an equivalent for the Polish word *Żal!*—and, his ear seeming to relish the sound, he repeated it frequently. It comprehends the entire gamut of emotions produced by a profound *regret*, from repentance to hatred, fruits blessed or envenomed by this acrid root.

Żal! a strange substantive, with a strange diversity and a stranger philosophy! Susceptible of varying applications,

79

it encloses all the tenderness and all the humility of a resigned and unmurmuring regret as long as its direct application is to facts and things and, so to speak, yields gently to the law of beneficent fate. But changing appearance and bowing to indirect governance, as soon as it applies to man it signals the ferment of malice, the revolt of censure, and the foretaste of vengeance, with threats implacably growling in the depths of the heart or feeding upon sterile bitterness as it espies revenge!

And in truth, *Żal!* constantly colors the whole output of Chopin's works with a reflection sometimes glowing and sometimes silvery. It is not absent from even his sweetest musings, those in which Berlioz, the Shakespearean genius who embraces all extremes, so clearly glimpsed *divine endearments*—wheedling ways natural only to women of semi-Oriental lands, ways in which men are rocked by their mothers, indulged by their sisters and enchanted by their mistresses, which later make the blandishments of other women seem vapid or coarse and give rise to the wholly justified boast: *Niema iak Polki!* [Polish women are unequalled!][3] The secret of these *divine endearments* makes these creatures adorable. They alone can fulfill the passionate dreams of poets who, like M. de Chateaubriand, in the feverish sleeplessness of youth, create a demoness and a charmer, and they find only one resemblance to their impossible visions "of an Eve, innocent and fallen, knowing all and nothing, virgin yet

3. The earlier custom of drinking from her own shoe the health of the woman to be especially honored is one of the most original traditions of enthusiastic Polish gallantry.

lover!!!"[4] in a Polish girl of sixteen, "half odalisque and half Valkyrie . . . feminine fusion of all age and beauty, realization of ancient sylph . . . Flora anew. . . ."[5] freed from the yoke of the seasons, and whom M. de Chateaubriand feared to see again! Divine endearments, generous and grudging at the same time, impressing upon the enamored heart the uncertain and lulling rocking of a boat with neither oars nor rigging.

In his performance Chopin delightfully imparted that sense of restlessness that gave the melody a surging effect, like a skiff on the crest of a mighty wave. Early in his writings he described this style, which lent such an individual stamp to his playing, by the phrase *Tempo rubato:* time stolen or broken, a flexible measure, both lingering and abrupt, quivering like a breath-shaken flame. In his later publications he ceased to do this, convinced that if its meaning were understood, it would be impossible to ignore this rule of irregularity. Thus all of his pieces should be played with this measured and accented alternation, the secret of which is difficult to grasp unless he himself was frequently heard. He seemed eager to teach this style to his many pupils, especially his compatriots to whom, more than to others, he wished to impart his method of performance. It was the women among them rather than the men who grasped it with that sympathy which they hold for all things relating to sentiment and poetry, and an instinctive understanding of his thought allowed them to follow all the shiftings of his azured yearning.

4. *Mémoires d'outre-tombe,* Vol. I: *Incantation.*
5. *Ibid.,* Vol. III: *Atala.*

4

IN CONCERT AND AT HOME

We HAVE SPOKEN of the composer and of his works, alive with deathless feelings, wherein his genius grappled with sorrow—and one of art's missions is to reconcile this fearful factor of reality with heaven—and struggled sometimes as conqueror, sometimes as victim. We have spoken of his works into which are poured (like tears streaming into a weeping-urn) all the memories of his youth, all the inclinations of his heart, all the ardor of his secret motivations and desires—of works that reach into the world of Dryads, Oreads, and Oceanides, and we find our sensitivity too blunted to follow, our perception too dulled to absorb. We should now speak of his performance ability if we had the sad courage to do so, if we could revive emotions entwined with our most intimate recollections and paint their memories with the colors they demand. But we feel it useless, for what result could our efforts produce? Would they, to those who did not hear him, communicate the charm of an unutterable poesy, subtle and pervasive like one of those delicate and exotic fragrances of the Ethiopian calla or verbena which are only perceptible in uncrowded space and, as if frightened, are dissipated in dense throngs where the thickening air retains only the penetrating odor of full-blown tuberoses or of burning resin?

Chopin knew that his talent—in style and imagination recalling Nodier, through purity of delivery, through familiarity with *La Fée aux miettes* and *Les Lutins d'Argail*, through echoes of *Séraphines* and *Dianes* whispering their most confidential laments and most secret dreams—Chopin knew, we insist, that he had no effect upon the multitude and could not strike the masses. They are like a sea of lead and no less heavy to move, their waves are stirred by fire. They need the strong arm of the stalwart laborer to be spilled into a mold where the flowing metal suddenly assumes thought and feeling in accordance with the imposed form. He knew that he was completely appreciated only in those too-rare gatherings where all the hearers were ready to follow and accompany him into those spheres that the ancients entered solely through an ivory gate surrounded by diamond pilasters crowned by domes, where all prismatic rays play upon a fawny crystal, such as the Mexican opal, its kaleidoscopic foci being hidden in an olive-colored mist that covers and discovers them by turn—spheres where all is entrancing magic, mad surprise, dream made manifest, and where Chopin so willingly sought refuge and delight. He spoke thus one day to an artist friend who has since been heard a great deal:

"I am not fitted to give concerts, the public frightens me, I feel suffocated by its panting breath, paralyzed by its curious glance, mute before those unknown faces; but you are destined for it, for when you do not win the public you are able to overwhelm it."

Aware of the conditions imposed by the nature of his talent, he played but rarely in public, and except for a few beginning concerts in 1831, when he was heard in Vienna and Munich, he played thereafter only in Paris. He was unable to travel on account of his health, which was so feeble that for months on end he was at the point of dying. On his only journey to the south, in the hope that a gentler climate would benefit him, his condition was so alarming that the innkeepers more than once demanded full payment for the bed and mattresses he had used in order to burn them afterward. They believed that he was already at that stage of consumption which is so readily contagious.

However, if we may venture the opinion, we believe that those concerts tired his physical constitution less than they did his artistic sensibility. His voluntary sacrifice of clamorous success concealed, we think, an internal hurt. He had a very clear sense of his great superiority, but perhaps its echo and reverberation did not suffice to bring him the quiet certainty that he was fully appreciated. Popular acclamation was wanting, and he doubtless wondered to what degree the distinguished salons compensated, in the enthusiasm of their applause, for the general public that he avoided. Few understood him, but did these few understand him sufficiently? A discontent, perhaps quite indefinite in his mind, at least with respect to its true source, secretly undermined him. He was obviously almost shocked by eulogy. What he was entitled to claim did not arrive in great outbursts, and he was inclined to be vexed by isolated praises. He often brushed them off, like annoying dust, with polite remarks, and these made it quickly evident that he felt not only slightly applauded but badly applauded, that he preferred to be undisturbed in his solitude and sentiment.

Much too subtle an expert in jesting and too clever in derision to expose himself to sarcasm, he assumed no attitude of misunderstood genius. Happily complacent in outward appearance, he so completely hid the injury to his rightful pride that its existence was scarcely suspected. But the gradually increasing rarity of his concerts[1] could be attributed, not unreasonably, more to his desire to avoid occasions that failed to bring him deserved tributes than to his frailty, which was roughly tested by continuous teaching and long hours of private playing.

Unfortunately the undoubted advantages for an artist that result from a selective audience are lessened by the meagerness of its sympathies. The *chill* that covers its gracious approval, like fruit topping a dessert, and the unruffled calm that governs the expression of its warmest enthusiasm could not content him. Torn from his lonely inspiration, the poet can only regain it in the livelier, more responsive, and more attentive interest of his listeners. He

1. Some years went by without his giving any, and we believe that his concert of 1844, in Pleyel's salons, followed a ten-year interruption.

will never succeed in drawing it from the cold glances of an areopagus assembled, so to speak, to judge him. His is the task to arouse and move those who listen, his feelings awakening similar feelings as he bids them to follow at last in his journey toward the infinite—as the chief of a wingèd band, giving the sign of departure, is followed by all his charges toward more lovely shores.

But had conditions been different—had Chopin collected the full share of homage and exalted admiration that he so richly deserved; had he been heard, like so many others, in all countries and climes; had he gained those flashing triumphs which create a shrine wherever people hail merit, honor, and genius; had he been known and acknowledged by thousands instead of merely by hundreds, we should not be pausing at this part of his career to detail his success.

What are bouquets to those whose brow clamors for immortal laurel? Fleeting sympathies and passive praises are scarcely to be mentioned beside a tomb that greater glories claim. Chopin's creations are destined to convey into distant years and lands those joys and comforts and warm emotions that works of art awaken in suffering souls, worn and fainting or persevering and believing. Dedicated to them, they thus establish an unbroken bond among lofty spirits on whatever hillside or in whatever period they may have lived, in keeping silent ill divined by their contemporaries and in speaking often misunderstood!

"There are different crowns," said Goethe; "some may even be gathered while taking a stroll." These latter can charm momentarily by their fragrant freshness, but we cannot range them with what Chopin laboriously won through ceaseless, matchless work, through an earnest love of art, and through a grievous sensing of the emotions that he so well expressed.

Since he sought not with a paltry greed those easy crowns which more than one of us has the modesty to boast of; since he lived as a man pure and generous, kind and compassionate, filled with a single sentiment, the noblest one on earth, feeling for fatherland; since he passed among us like a phantom consecrated by all of Polish poesy, let us beware of failing to revere his grave. Let us toss there no wreath of artificial flowers, no slight and facile crowns! Before this coffin let us raise our hearts! Let us learn from him to cast out all but the noblest ambitions, to concentrate our concerns on efforts that dig a deeper furrow than the fashion of the day! Let us renounce, too, for ourselves, in the dreary time in which we live, all that is unworthy of art, all that lacks permanence, all that fails to shelter some grain of eternal and immaterial beauty which art must lighten gloriously in order to glow itself, and let us remember the ancient prayer of the Dorians, whose simple formula was so reverently poetic when they petitioned the gods: *to give them Good through Beauty!* Instead of laboring so to attract and please listeners at any price, let us rather strive, like Chopin, to leave a celestial echo of what we have felt, loved, and endured! And finally let us learn from that memory to demand of ourselves whatever ennobles in the mystical city of art rather than to seek from the present, without regard to the future, those easy crowns which, scarce assumed, are at once dulled and forgotten!

Instead of these, the fairest tributes that an artist can receive during his lifetime were tendered to Chopin by *glorious equals,* and an enthusiastic admiration was pledged to him by a public still more restricted than the musical aristocracy that appeared at his concerts. It consisted of a group of celebrated names, and their owners bowed before him like kings of divers empires assembled to fête a colleague. They paid him unreservedly the honor that was his, and in France this was inevitable—where hospitality can sensitively perceive the true worth of her guests.

The most distinguished minds of Paris met often in Chopin's salon; not, it is true in those artists' meetings of fancied regularity such as the idle imagination of some ceremonially bored circles dream up and such as have never been, for high spirits, zest, liveliness, and enthusiasm come to no one at an appointed hour and perhaps even less to genuine artists—all more or less infected by the *divine complaint* of which they must shake off the benumbing paralysis, forget the chilling pains in order to lose themselves and revel in those glittering games that astonish dumfounded onlookers who from time to time glimpse a Roman candle, a rosy flash of fireworks, a cascade of streaming flame, or a harmless frightening dragon. For poets and artists, too, unfortunately, only encounter gaiety and animation by chance! Some of them, it is true, are more privileged. They have the happy gift either of mastering inner pain in order to bear their burden ever lightly and to laugh with their fellow travelers at the troubles of the road, or of preserving a kind and gentle calm which, like a mute token of hope and comfort, revives, uplifts, and spurs them on. While they stay within this tranquil air, it gives them a vital freedom of mind that can become the more intensive as it contrasts with their sullenness, their tedium, and their care.

Chopin really belonged to neither group, yet he had that instinctive grace of Polish welcome which not only observes the laws and duties of hospitality, but, even more, forgets every personal consideration in bowing to the desires and pleasures of invited guests. It was delightful to visit him. Those who came to his quarters were enchanted and put at ease, everything was at their disposal, and he and all he possessed were theirs to command—unlimited generosity which even the simple Slavic laborer never failed to practice in offering the honors of his hut, more joyously eager than the Arab in his tent, compensating for any lack in the splendor of his reception by an adage which he never tired of repeating (repeated also by the great lord following a feast of exquisite luxury served in a gilded palace): *Czym bohal, tym rad.* For strangers this is paraphrased so: "Deign to pardon what is unworthy of you, but I place at your feet all my humble wealth!"[2] This formula, uttered with a national grace and dignity,

2. The polite address of the Pole is strongly marked by the exaggerated characteristics of Oriental speech. The appellations *most powerful* and *most enlightened Lord* are still obligatory. *Benefactor [Dobrodzij]* is regularly used in conversation, and the common greeting between men or of man speaking to woman is: *I fall at your feet [Padam do nog]*; the greeting of the people has an ancient simplicity and solemnness: *Glory to God [Slawa Bohu].*

is spoken to guests by every family head who preserves the delicate, picturesque customs of Poland's ancient ways.

After familiarity with the exercise of Polish hospitality our meetings in Chopin's dwelling can be better imagined, with their expansiveness, lack of restraint, and good fellowship, qualities that leave no flat or bitter aftertaste and awaken no tinge of ill feeling. Although he obviously avoided society, he displayed a charming warmth when guests entered his salon. While appearing to center his attention on no one, he succeeded in treating everybody most congenially and demonstrated to each a zealous devotion.

Undoubtedly Chopin had some slightly misanthropic prejudices to overcome in opening his door and his piano to those whose friendship, as respectful as it was loyal, allowed such an earnest request. More than one of us surely remember that first improvised evening with him, in spite of his refusal, when he was living in the Chaussée d'Antin.

His apartment, unexpectedly overrun, was lighted by only a few candles gathered around one of those Pleyel pianos that he specially favored because of their silvery, somewhat veiled, tone and easy touch. It permitted him to draw therefrom sounds that might recall one of those harmonicas of which romantic Germany held the monopoly and which her ancient masters so ingeniously constructed by joining water and crystal.

Corners left in darkness seemed to remove the limits of the room and to extend it into the shadows of space.

In a play of light and shade, clothed in a whitish slip-cover, a piece of furniture could be seen; vague in outline, it stood like a specter come to hear the sounds that had called it forth. The light concentrated around the piano fell on the floor, gliding over the surface like a spreading wave and mingling with the flickering gleamings of the hearth where, from time to time, orange-colored flames, short and broad, shot up like curious gnomes summoned by words in their own tongue. A single portrait—of a pianist, an admiring, sympathetic friend—seemed called to be the constant listener to the ebb and flow of tone that moaned and growled, murmured and expired on and about the surface of the nearby instrument. By weird chance the responding surface of the mirror, duplicating the image for us, reflected only the handsome oval face and the silky blond curls which so many brushes have copied, which the burin has just reproduced for those who are charmed by an elegant pen.

Assembled around the piano in the lighted area were several figures of brilliant renown: Heine, saddest of humorists, listening with the interest of a compatriot to the tales that Chopin told him, tales about the mysterious land that also haunted his airy fancy since he had explored its most delightful parts. By mere suggestion of word and tone he and Chopin understood each other, and the musician answered with surprising phrases the questions that the poet softly asked about those unknown regions, even about that "laughing nymph"[3] of whom he sought

3. Heine, Salon, *Chopin*.

news, inquiring "whether she continued to drape her silver veil over her green-hued hair with the same saucy coquetry?" During the chattering and amorous accounts about those places he wanted to know "if that sea-god with the long white beard still pursued a certain pert and roguish naiad with his ludicrous love?" Well-informed on all the glorious enchantments that are seen *yonder, yonder,* he would ask "if the roses there still glowed with so proud a flame? if the trees there still sang so harmoniously in the moonlight?" Chopin would reply, and both, after talking long and intimately of the charms of that aerial country, would fall silent in the throes of nostalgia. This affected Heine so when he compared himself to that Dutch captain of the *phantom ship,* with his crew eternally tossed on the chilling waves and "vainly sighing for the spices, tulips, hyacinths, meerschaum pipes and porcelain cups of Holland—'*Amsterdam! Amsterdam! when shall we again see Amsterdam!*' they cry, while the tempest roared in the rigging and swung them hither and yon over the watery hell." "I understand," added Heine, "the fury with which the unfortunate captain one day exclaimed: '*Oh! if I ever return to Amsterdam, I should rather become a boundary mark at the corner of one of its streets than ever leave them again!*' Poor Van der Deken!"

Heine knew full well all that poor Van der Deken had suffered and experienced in his terrible, endless race across the sea, which had seized in its clutches the wood of his unstained ship, holding it close to her tossing bosom by an invisible anchor—and he could never find the chain in order to snap the bond. When so inclined he would tell us of the sorrows and hopes, the despairs and tortures, the dejection of the unfortunates on board the cheerless boat, for he had mounted its accursed decks, guided and led by the hand of some enamored water sprite. When the guest of her coral glade and pearly palace arose more sullen and sharp and bitter than usual, she would offer him between repasts, to brighten his ill humor, a spectacle worthy of that lover who could dream of more extravagancies than her kingdom contained.

On this deathless ship he had crossed the poles where the aurora borealis, flashing visitor of protracted nights, brushes its broad scarf over the enormous stalactites of eternal ice. He had entered the tropics where, at times of abbreviated darkness, the triangle of the zodiac replaces with its ineffable light the burning flames shot out of a torturing sun. He had crossed those latitudes where life is oppressed and where it is devoured, and on the way he learned to recognize all the heavenly marvels that mark the route of sailors without a port. Lodged in the rudderless stern, he had scanned the skies, from the two Bears majestically dominating the North to the brilliant Southern Cross beyond which is the antarctic desert, stretching overhead and underfoot. It leaves the bewildered eye nothing to view in an empty, unmarked sky spread above a shoreless sea. He had long followed in the blue the momentary path of shooting stars, like fireflies far above, and those comets of unpredictable orbit, feared for their strange splendor though their aimless, lonely journeys are only sad and harmless—and Aldebaran, that distant star which, like the ominous spark of a hostile glance, seems to watch our globe without venturing to draw nigh—and those radiant planets shedding on the searching, restless eye a light that warms and comforts like a quizzical promise.

Heine had seen all of these things, their appearance differing in each meridian, and he had seen many other things besides, describing them in terms of vague semblance. He had witnessed Herodias' wild cavalcade, had entered the court of the King of the Elves and the garden of the Hesperides, had penetrated into all those places inaccessible to mortals having no fairy godmother who strives, during their life, to compensate for ill fortune by lavishing on them her treasures.

Seated beside Heine the evening we speak of was Meyerbeer, who has long since exhausted all admiring exclamations. Harmonist of cyclopean structures, he passed long moments of rare delight as he followed the detail of arabesques enwrapping Chopin's thoughts as in a light translucence.

Farther away sat Adolphe Nourrit, that noble artist who was both ardent and ascetic, a devout and well-nigh austere Catholic. He dreamed of the future with medieval fervor, and in his final years he refused his talent to all scenes of shallow sentiment. He served art with a chaste and burning awe, accepting it in its varied guises and viewing it every waking hour as a holy tabernacle *the beauty of which formed the glory of the true.* His brow was creased by a melancholy passion for the beautiful.

Already it seemed marbled by that doomful shade that the outburst of despair always explains too late to men so avid for the secrets of the heart but so clumsy in divining them.

Hiller was also there. His talent was related to Chopin's, and he was one of his most faithful friends. We often gathered in his own apartment, and while waiting for the great compositions he published subsequently (the first being his remarkable oratorio *The Destruction of Jerusalem*) he would write piano pieces. Some of them, entitled *Études*, are vigorous sketches of polished design. They recall those studies of foliage in which landscapists perchance bring forth a complete little poem of shadow and light in a single tree, a single branch, a single line happily and freely treated.

Eugène Delacroix remained silent and absorbed in the specters that filled the air, their rustlings seemingly audible to all. Was he wondering what palette, what brushes, what canvas he should have chosen to quicken them into life by his art? Was he pondering on a fabric woven by Arachne, a brush made of fairy eyelashes, and a palette covered with rainbow mists that he would have to unveil? Was he pleased to smile inwardly at these fancies and to surrender himself wholly to the impression that gave them birth, through the attraction that some great talents feel for others of contrasting nature?

The one among us who appeared nearest to the grave was the elderly Niemcevicz, and he listened to the *historic lays* that Chopin dramatically translated for this survivor of bygone times. Under his fingers and alongside the highly popular themes of the Polish bard were heard the clash of arms, the song of conquerors, the festal hymns, the plaints of famous captives, and the ballads of perished heroes. Together they recalled the long succession of glories, victories, kings, queens, hetmans—and the old man, taking the present for illusion, believed them all revived. Apart from all the others, dark and silent, Mickiewicz presented his motionless silhouette. The Dante of the North, he always seemed to find "the salt of the Stranger bitter, and his stairway hard to climb."

Deep in an armchair, her arms on a console, Mme Sand was curiously enrapt and becomingly subdued. She brought to her listening the full power of her ardent genius, which had the rare quality, reserved only for a few elect, of perceiving beauty in any form of art and nature, a quality that might be that *second sight* the superior gifts of which all nations acknowledge in women who are inspired. An entranced stare enables their vision to penetrate the bark, the covering, the coarse wrapping of form and permits them to glimpse, in its invisible essence, the soul there incarnated, the ideal that the poet and artist have conjured up under the swirl of notes or layers of color, the folds of marble, the shaping of stone or the mysterious rhythms of verse. It is a quality dimly apprehended by most; its supreme manifestation, revealed in a divining oracle aware of the past and prophesying the future, is much less common than is imagined. It is a quality that rids those fortunate enough to possess it of the cumbersome burden of technical science, sluggishly pushing toward the esoteric regions that they win to spontaneously—a quality that takes wing far less in the secrets of science than in a frequent communing with Nature.

In the practice of these encounters with Creation lie the attraction and nobility of rural life. Here is best caught the message it conceals in the infinite harmonies of shapes and sounds, of lights, of tumult and twitter, of terror and sensuousness—overwhelming combinations which, tested and confronted by a courage that no mystery or delay can weaken or weary, sometimes grants a glimpse of the key to analogies and conformities, to the relations of our meanings and feelings. They allow us to know simultaneously both the hidden ties that bind apparent dissimilarities, identical opposites, and equivalent antitheses, and the chasms which separate, by a narrow but unbridgeable space, that which is destined to draw close without merging, to resemble without mingling. As with Mme Sand, an early listening to those whisperings whereby Nature initiates her favored ones into her mystic rites is one of the attributes of the poet. Learning from Nature to dream as man does, as he in turn creates and (in works of all kinds) handles the tumult and twitter, the terror and sensuousness, is a still more subtle gift, and Mme Sand, as woman and poet, possessed it doubly through the intuition of her heart and her genius.

Having named her whose energetic personality and flashing genius inspired in Chopin's frail and delicate nature an admiration that consumed him as a too-heady wine destroys too-fragile vases, we can summon no other names from the limbo of the past where float so many blurred pictures and sympathies, dubious plans and beliefs, where each of us could see again the outline of some stillborn feeling! Alas! of the interests and inclinations and desires that filled a period when elevated souls and shining minds were fortuitously thrown together, how many had sufficient vitality to survive all the causes of death that surround each thought and emotion as they do each person in the cradle? How many are there of which, at some moment in their more or less brief existence, this word of matchless sorrow has not been uttered: *Happy if dead! happier if never born!* Of so many feelings that made noble hearts beat high, how many are there that were never exposed to this curse supreme? Perhaps not a single one, if rekindled from its ash and issued from its grave (like the suicide lover in Mickiewicz' poem who returns from the dead to relive his life and to resuffer his griefs) would appear without the scars and bruises and disfigurements that marred its original beauty and sullied its simplicity. And among these gloomy specters how many would be found whose beauty and simplicity might have held enchantments of sufficient power and heavenly radiance to obviate the fear, after fading and expiring, of being disowned by those who joyed and suffered in them? What a funeral roll call would not be essential to call them forth one by one, asking what they produced of good and ill in the world of emotions where they received such liberal shelter, in the heart-governed world they adorned—upset, illumined, and stricken according to their caprice.

But if among the men forming those groups, each one of whom attracted the attention of many souls and bore in his conscience the goad of many responsibilities, there is one who has not permitted the purity of the natural charm binding them into a radiant sheaf to lapse into forgetfulness; one who, dropping from his memory the fermentations that the sweetest perfumes are prone to, has bequeathed to art only the full inheritance of his most rapt loftiness and his most inspired ecstasies—let us hail him as one predestined, whose popular poesy attests existence through its faith in *good genii*. Has the attribution to these creatures (supposedly beneficent to men) of a nature above the common not been magnificently confirmed by a great Italian poet who defined genius as "a stronger impress of Divinity"? Let us bow before all who have been thus more deeply marked by the mystic seal; but let us especially revere, with an intimate tenderness, those like Chopin, who exercised that supremacy only to give life and expression to the most beautiful emotions.

5

INTEGRITY AND INDIVIDUALITY
CLASSICISM AND ROMANTICISM

A NATURAL CURIOSITY centers around the lives of men who have dedicated great talents to the glorification of noble feelings in works of art where they shine like resplendent meteors before the amazed and delighted throng. The crowd willingly associates the admiring, sympathetic impressions thus awakened with their names, which it would promptly accept as a symbol of nobleness and greatness. It is tempting to believe that those who can so eloquently express and voice these sentiments must know no others. But this kindly prejudice and favorable presumption need to be justified by those to whom they apply and to be supported by their lives. When in his work the poet's heart is caught reacting, with such exquisite delicacy, to sweet inspiration, divining in a flash of intuition what is veiled by pride or timid modesty or vexing bitterness, caught painting the love of youthful dreams and of later desperation—when his genius is observed mastering such grand situations, rising calmly above all the vicissitudes of human destiny, finding in the entanglement of its unsolvable knots the threads that triumphantly and proudly free it, soaring above all manner of grandeur and disaster, climbing toward the summits that others no longer reach—when he is known to hold the secret of the most subtle shades of tenderness and the most imposing forms of stark courage—how evade the question: Is this marvelous insight the miracle of a deep belief in these feelings or is it a clever abstraction of thought and a play of the mind?

How can the query be avoided: In what way have these men, so in love with the beautiful, made their lives different from those of ordinary beings? How was that poetic splendor maintained as it struggled with the realities and material interests of life? To what extent were those ineffable emotions of love actually independent of the usually poisonous mildews and acerbities? To what extent were they protected from that frivolity and inconstancy that lead to their neglect? Other queries: Were they always just who felt such righteous indignation? Those who exalted integrity, did they never traffic with their conscience? Were those who sang of honor never timorous? Were those who vaunted bravery never compromised by their weakness?

There are many eager to know the relationships between honor, loyalty, and fineness, and the gains and advantages only won at their expense, which are admitted by those entrusted with the noble task of sustaining our faith and affection for great and lofty feelings by giving them life in art when they had no refuge elsewhere. For many, a denial of these relationships would be impossible or foolish. Thus when some unfortunate examples lend their words a lamentable support, how promptly do they call the poet's loveliest conceptions vain deceits! what wisdom they flaunt in preaching doctrines, knowingly premeditated, of a honeyed and ruthless hypocrisy, of a continual and hidden contradiction between words and actions! With what cruel joy do they cite these examples to weak and disturbed souls whose youthful aspirations (or dwindling forces and convictions) still endeavor to elude these mournful compacts! What fatal depression seizes these latter before the harsh alternatives and beguiling interventions encountered at every turn on the road of life! They are persuaded that hearts most passionately enamored of sublimity, most skilled in delicate susceptibilities, most affected by the beauties of simplicity have, nevertheless, by their acts, denied the objects of their worship and their song! What agonizing doubts must grasp and consume them as they face these flagrant contradictions! And what mockery is showered upon their sufferings by those who repeat: *Poetry is that which might have been*—and who rejoice to blaspheme it by this guilty negation! For Poetry is no mere shadow of our Imagination, cast and magnified beyond measure on the soaring plane of the Impossible; for "Poetry and Reality" [*Dichtung und*

Wahrheit] are not two incompatible elements destined to brush each other and never join together: so the opinion of Goethe, who said of a contemporary poet that "having lived to create poems, he had made a poem of his life" [*Er lebte dichtend und dichtete lebend*]. Goethe himself was too much a poet not to realize that Poetry exists only because it finds its eternal Reality in the finest instincts of a human heart.

Like nobility, *Génie oblige*, as we once had occasion to say.[1] If the example of the cold austerity of unbending disinterestedness of certain characters can win the admiration of calm and collected natures, where will the more passionate and the more easily moved find their models, those who see every drab environment as vapid and who eagerly seek either the joys of honor or pleasures, purchased regardless of price? These beings gladly shake off the yoke of senile authorities. They reject their competence. They accuse them of monopolizing the world on behalf of their withered passions, to further the effects of causes that elude them, and of proclaiming laws in spheres they are unable to enter! They turn their questioning gaze toward others—they query those who have drunk at the boiling spring of grief, gushing from the foot of slopes where the soul builds itself an eyrie. They pass beyond the somber silence of those who practice the good without exalting the beautiful. Does ardent youth have leisure to interpret silence, to resolve its problems? Its heart races too madly to perceive the hidden sufferings, the mysterious

1. Speaking of Paganini, after his death.

fights and lonely struggles that are sometimes lodged in the upright man's quiet glance. Stormy souls understand ill the calm simplicity of the just or the heroic smile of stoicism. They demand enthusiasm and emotion. The picture will persuade them, metaphor carry conviction, and tears their proof—and they prefer the finality of contagion to the weariness of argument. They turn with avid curiosity to the poets and artists who have stirred them by image, swept them on by metaphor, inflamed them by outburst. They ask from them the full measure of these passions and explosions.

When, in those wretched hours fraught with torment, they become a heavy, cumbersome treasure, ready to cause shipwreck if not thrown overboard into the depth of forgetfulness, who, having braved their dangers and felt the threat of disaster, has not called upon the glorious shades and spirits to determine the sincerity and sturdiness of their aspirations, to inquire with clever discrimination what was only an amusement, what a conjecture of the mind, and what formed the firm base of their feeling? It is in such hours that disparagement is not idle. It seizes greedily upon the faults and weakness and negligence of those who have excoriated faults and weakness. It overlooks nothing. It grasps its prey, probes shortcomings, and assumes a right of scorn over inspiration, according it no other purpose than providing entertainment and denying it the power to guide our actions, and resolutions, our assent or our refusal. Disparagement, mocking and cynical, knows how to winnow history! Dropping the good grain, it carefully gathers the bad in order to scatter its black seed over the brilliant pages that bear the heart's purest desires and imagination's noblest dreams. And with victorious irony it asks: What is this pure grain that flowers only in famine? What are these vain words that beget only sterile emotion? To what purpose these excursions in a realm where no fruit is plucked? Of what worth are these feelings and ardors which end only in calculated interest and harbor only the interest of self?

With what arrogant derision does disparagement draw together and view the poet's noble outburst and unworthy abasement! the artist's lovely song and guilty levity! What superiority it assumes over the solid virtues of *worthy* people (whom it likens to shellfish, fated to know only the immobility of lower systems) and over the pompous elation of those presumably better who fail to renounce, even as well as the others, the pursuit of material comfort, satisfactions of vanity, and immediate pleasures! What advantage does it not assume in the logical agreement of its pursuits and rejections? How smartly it triumphs over the hesitations and doubts and aversions of those who would still believe possible the union of vivid feeling, ardent impression, quick intelligence, and poetic meaning with upright character, unblemished life, and conduct that never belies the poetic ideal!

How then escape the noblest sadness whenever a deed shows the poet disobedient to the inspiration of the Muses, talent's guardian angels, who would so want to teach him to make his life his finest poem? What dismaying skepticism, what lamentable dejection, what grievous apostasies the genius' lapses carry in their train! Yet that voice would cry sacrilege that, in one anathema, would confuse these deviations with boasting depravity and crawling baseness. It would cry sacrilege! for if the poet's action has some-times belied his song, has not his song still better denied his deed? And may not his work contain virtues that are stronger than his behavior is noxious? Evil is contagious, but good is fertile! Yielding his convictions before the indulgence unworthy of his nature, the poet has not less glorified the feelings that condemn him and that, per-meating his works, give them a sway far more reaching than his private life exerts. Have not these works comforted and calmed and edified more souls than the vacillations of his dismal course have battered? Art is mightier than the artist. His creations have a life independent of his un-steady will, for they are a manifestation of immutable beauty and, more lasting than he, they traverse generation after generation, whole and incorruptible, holding the veritable power of the artist's redemption.

If, alas, there be some who have immortalized their aspirations and their sensitivity by giving them the com-manding influence of an irresistible eloquence, but have stifled those aspirations and abused that sensitivity, how many must they have inwardly strengthened, confirmed, and encouraged in a noble path by their works of genius! Indulgence alone, perhaps, would be their justice; but how hard it is to summon justice! how repugnant to be forced to defend what should be admired, to excuse what should be revered!

What sweet pride the friend and artist experience in recalling a career free of wounding clashes, free of pardoned contradictions, free of errors excusable only in tracing their source, free of extremes that are pitied as the result of many causes. With what sweet pride do they name one who has discovered that listless natures are not alone exempt from fascinations and illusions, who works with ease within firm strictures and the common limitations of honored and honorable laws, maintaining that spiritual elevation that acknowledges no reverse or ever a self-betrayal! In this respect the memory of Chopin will remain doubly dear to the friends and artists he encountered on his path, and likewise to the unknown friends who were won by the poet's songs and to the artists coming after, who will gain glory in being worthy of him!

In none of its many manifestations did Chopin's character harbor a single emotion, a single impulse, which was not dictated by the most delicate sense of honor and the noblest understanding of the affections. And yet there never was a nature more inclined to eccentricity, whim, and abrupt caprice. His imagination was passionate, his feelings tended toward violence: his physical system was weak and sickly. Who can measure the sufferings proceeding from such contrasts? They were surely heart-rending, but he never exposed them to view! He kept them hidden, screened from all glances, beneath the impenetrable calm of proud resignation.

The frailness of his heart and constitution forced upon him the feminine martyrdom of tortures never admitted, and weighted his destiny with certain features of feminine fate. Shut out by health from the breathless arena of general activity, with no liking for that useless buzzing of bees and hornets joining together to vent their surplus energy, he built himself a cell removed from too-worn and too-trodden paths. No adventures or complexities or episodes spotted a life that he made simple, although he was surrounded by circumstances apt to render such a goal difficult of attainment. Events for him were feelings and impressions, more striking and important than external shifts and happenings. The lessons that he gave, constantly, regularly, and assiduously, were his daily and domestic obligation, discharged with satisfaction and in good conscience. He unburdened his soul in composition as others do in prayer, pouring out those effusions of the heart, those unexpressed sorrows, those indescribable griefs that devout souls spill in their talks with God. He told in his works what they tell only on bended knee: those mysteries of passion and pain which man has been permitted to understand without words because he cannot express them in words.

The care that Chopin exercised in avoiding the—if we may use the word—zigzag of life's pattern, in shunning its excrescences and the crumbling of aimless, formless particles, prevented the accumulation of incident. A few blurred lines enwrap his image as if in bluish smoke, vanishing under the finger that would touch or trace it. He took part in no activity, no drama, no alliance, and no issue. He wielded a decisive influence over no person. His will never encroached upon any desire. He neither fettered nor controlled any mind through the domination of his own. He tyrannized over no heart, he laid no conquering hand on any fate—he sought nothing, and would have scorned to ask for aught. Like Tasso he could say:

Brama assai, poco spera, e nulla chiede.[2]

But he also eluded all bonds and all friendships that would have dragged him in their train and thrust him into stormier spheres. Ready to give all, he never gave himself. Perhaps he knew what exclusive devotion, what unlimited affection he might have worthily inspired, worthily understood and shared! Perhaps he thought, like certain aspiring souls, that if love and friendship are not all, they are nothing! Perhaps it cost him more effort to accept a share thereof than never to have savored these feelings and to have known only a hopeless ideal! No one knows exactly if this is the way he was, for he barely mentioned love or friendship. He was not exacting, like those whose rights and just demands would far exceed what might be offered them. His closest acquaintances failed to penetrate to that sacred retreat where his soul dwelt, apart from the rest of his life—a retreat so hidden that it was scarce suspected.

In his relations and conversations he appeared concerned only with what interested others; he refrained from imposing his own personality upon theirs. Of the small amount of time he spared them, at least he kept none for himself. Whatever he might have dreamed, whatever he

2. "Loved much, hoped little, and desired nought," from *Gerusalemme liberata* (tr. Edward Fairfax), Bk. II, st. 16.—*Trans.*

might have wished or wanted or won, whether his white and slender hand could have adapted strings of brass to his lyre's golden cords, no one ever asked him, and in his presence no one would have had opportunity to think thereof. His talk dealt rarely with emotional topics. He glided over them, and since he was ungenerous with his time, his remarks were readily exhausted in the happenings of the day. He was careful, moreover, not to let his words slip into digressions of which he might become the subject. His individuality scarcely prompted the investigation of curiosity, probing thoughts and searching guile. His way was too pleasing to incur reflection. His whole being was harmonious and seemed to require no comment. The blue of his eye was more animated than dreamy; his fine and gentle smile did not shift to bitterness. The delicacy and transparency of his complexion caught the eye, his blond hair was silky, his nose slightly tilted, his bearing distinguished, and his manner had such an aristocratic stamp that he was instinctively treated like a prince. His gestures were many and graceful, the tone of his voice was always subdued and often dampened, he was small of stature and frail of limb. His entire appearance called to mind the morning-glory, swaying on stems incredibly fine and their cups so divinely colored, but of such a tenuous texture that the least touch would destroy them.

He carried into society the evenness of mood of persons who are undisturbed because they expect no advantage. He was customarily gay. His caustic mind quickly exposed the ridiculous far beyond the surface where it makes its impact. In pantomime he displayed a near-inexhaustible comic verve, and he often enjoyed reproducing, in farcical improvisation, the musical mannerisms and special idiosyncrasies of certain virtuosos, repeating their gestures and motions, and mimicking their face with a talent that betrayed their complete personality in a flash. At such times his features became unrecognizable as they underwent the most extraordinary changes. But while imitating the ugly and the grotesque he never lost his natural charm. Even grimace did not reach the point of disfiguring him, and his gaiety was the more piquant as he controlled its limits with perfect good taste, sensing the bounds it could not overstep. In all the moments of the closest intimacy he felt that an unbecoming word or an ill-timed sally might be shocking.

By a total exclusion of talk whereof he might be the subject, by constant discretion with regard to his own feelings, he always succeeded in leaving that impression so dear to ordinary people, the impression of a presence that charms without arousing fear that its favors must be paid for, that its flourish of contagious merriment must be followed by sadness of melancholy confidences and somber faces, those incvitable reactions of beings of whom it can be said: *Ubi mel ibi fel* [where there is honey there is gall]. And although the populace cannot withhold a kind of respect for the painful feelings that cause these reactions, exerting the attraction of the unknown and arousing something akin to admiration, they appreciate them only at a distance, and they flee their approach to dull tranquillity, just as ready to swoon at their description as to turn from their sight. Thus the presence of Chopin was always fêted —and he was so concerned with everything outside himself that his inward personality remained apart, unapproached and unapproachable beneath that smooth and polished surface where it was impossible to gain a foothold.

There were moments, however, admittedly rare, when we caught him very deeply affected. We saw him pale and blanch to such a point that his complexion turned greenish and cadaverous. But in his most violent emotions he retained self-control, and then he was usually reluctant to talk about what he resented. A minute of recovery always hid the secret of his immediate impression. The actions that followed thereafter, whatever spontaneous ease he could impart to them, were already the effect of a reflection and a will that mastered the strange conflict of moral energies and physical weaknesses gathered within him. This constant dominion wielded over the violence of his character recalled the sad superiority of beings who seek their strength in restraint and isolation, knowing the futility of explosive angers and too jealous of the mystery of their passions to betray it gratuitously.

He could forgive nobly, and no aftertaste of rancor remained in his heart for those who had hurt him. But as these hurts struck deep in his soul, they fermented there in undefined pain and inward suffering, to such a degree that long after their causes had vanished from memory he still felt their secret sting. Nevertheless, by dint of subjecting his feelings to what appeared to him as *ought to be* instead of *really is*, he became grateful for services proffered by friendship, better intentioned than instructed, that unsuspectingly crossed his hidden susceptibilities. These faults of awkwardness, however, are the most annoying for nervous temperaments to bear. They are condemned to control their rages and are brought thereby to a gnawing vexation which never acknowledges its true reasons and which would yet surely deceive those accepting it as eccentricity without reason. But since a disregard of what seemed to him the best course of conduct was a temptation he did not have to resist (for probably it never appeared), when confronted by personalities more energetic and thus more abrupt and decisive than his own, he refrained from showing the convulsive twitchings that their contact and association made him endure.

The reserve of his conversation extended to all the subjects that the fanaticism of opinion can fasten upon. He could be prejudged only by what he did not do in the narrow confines of his activity. His patriotism was revealed in the direction his talent followed, in his choice of friends, in his preference for pupils, in the frequent and considerable services that he liked to render his compatriots. We have no recollection, however, that he enjoyed expressing his feelings about it. If he talked occasionally about political ideas, so ceaselessly discussed in France, so sharply attacked and warmly defended, it was to point out what he thought was false and erroneous in them rather than to uphold other views. Having continuous contacts with some of the most noted political figures of the day, he could limit the relations between himself and them to a personal warmth wholly independent of conformity of thought.

In his eyes democracy represented a conglomeration of elements too heterogeneous, too distorted, too savagely powerful to win his sympathy. More than twenty years ago the entrance of social questions was compared to a new invasion of barbarians. Chopin was peculiarly and painfully struck by the terrible aspect of this phenomenon. He despaired of obtaining Rome's safety from these modern Attilas, of preserving from their destruction and devastation art and its monuments and effects—civilization, in a word, the elegant, refined and indolent life of which Horace sang. He followed events at a distance, and a hardly suspected perspicacity of vision led him to predict what better-informed persons little anticipated. If observations of this type slipped out, he did not develop them. His brief statements attracted attention only when the event had justified them. His good sense, extremely shrewd, had promptly convinced him of the complete emptiness of most political orations, theological discussions, and philosophical digressions. And so he began early to practice the favorite maxim of a highly distinguished man, a word we have oft heard repeated, dictated by the misanthropic wisdom of advanced years, a word that then astonished our innocent impatience but since has impressed us by its woeful rightness: "Some day you will be persuaded, as I am," said the Marquis Jules de Nailles to the young people whom he honored with his favors and who were caught in the heat of naïve discussions, "that there is scarcely any way of talking about anything with anyone."

A Catholic and truly religious, Chopin never approached this subject. He held to his beliefs without parading them. People could know him for a long time and gain no accurate idea of his thoughts on such matters. *Il mondo va da se,* he appeared to mutter in order to console his idle hand and reconcile it with his lute. We watched him for long periods amidst noisy and lively conversations from which he silently abstained. In the passion of the talkers he was forgotten; but for our part we often neglected to follow the thread of their reasoning so as to watch his countenance attentively. It would imperceptibly contract when he heard debated subjects dealing with the basic conditions of existence, the discussion being maintained so vigorously that our fates might have seemed to be awaiting immediate decision. He would appear to us then like a passenger on board a ship, tempest-tossed on the waves, watching the horizon and stars, thinking of his distant country, following the actions of the sailors, counting their mistakes, and all the while silent, lacking the requisite strength to grasp any of the rigging.

In one field only Chopin abandoned his calculated silence and his customary neutrality. He dropped his reserve in the cause of art. Here alone he would not surrender, under any condition, the explicit declaration of his judgment, and here he persistently endeavored to extend the effect of his influence and his will. This was like the tacit testimony of a great artist's authority which he felt he legitimately held for those questions arising from his skill and calling; and he never left doubt as to how he viewed them. For some years he injected a passionate zeal in his pleadings. Later, since the triumph of his ideas had lessened the interest of his rôle, he sought no further occasion to assume again the head of any faction. On the single occasion when he took a stand in a factional struggle, he gave proof of convictions that—rarely revealed like all deeply felt beliefs—were absolute, tenacious, and inflexible.

In 1832, shortly after his arrival in Paris, in music as in literature a new school was forming. Young talents were arising who lustily shook off the yoke of ancient formulas. The political agitation of the first years of the July revolution, scarcely allayed, was carried over with all its fervor to matters of literature and art that captured the attention and interest of the mind. *Romanticism* was the order of the day, and it was stubbornly contested, for and against. There was no truce between those who would not admit that writing could be different from what it had been previously and those who wanted the artist to be free to choose the form and mold it to his feeling, who thought that since the rule of form was based upon agreement with the emotion demanding utterance, each different mode of feeling necessarily sanctioned a different mode of expression. The former believed in the existence of a form that was permanent, its perception representing absolute beauty, and they judged each work from this pre-established point of view. But while admitting that the great Masters had attained the ultimate limits of art and supreme perfection, they left to the artists who followed no glory other than the hope to approach them, more or less by imitation; and they denied them even the hope of equaling them, since the perfecting of technic can never rise to the level of creation. The latter denied that beauty could have an unchanging, absolute form. The various forms as manifested in the history of art appeared to them as tents pitched along the road of the ideal, momentary points which the genius reaches from epoch to epoch and which his immediate successors must go beyond. The former wished to enclose in the symmetrical frame of similar patterns the inspirations of the most dissimilar times and kinds; the latter claimed for each inspiration the freedom to create their own style, and accepted no other rule than that which springs from the direct relations of feeling and form so that the one would answer for the other. (Existing models, however admirable, did not seem to have exhausted all the emotions that art can seize and all the forms that it can use.) Not stressing the excellence of form, they sought it only to the extent that its faultless perfection is indispensable to the full revelation of emotion, for they were aware that emotion is maimed as long as an imperfect form, like an opaque veil, intercepts its radiance. And so they subordinated professional craft to poetic inspiration, calling upon patience and genius to rejuvenate the form that would satisfy the demands of inspiration. They reproached their opponents for subjecting inspiration to Procrustean torture, for admitting that certain types of feeling were inexpressible in predetermined forms, and for depriving art in advance of all the works which would have tried to introduce new feelings in new shapes—feelings that come from the ever-progressing development of the human spirit and the instruments and material resources of art. Those who saw the flames of genius slowly consuming the old worm-eaten scaffolds rallied to the school of music of which Berlioz was the most gifted, most courageous, and most daring representative. Chopin joined wholeheartedly and was one of those who most perseveringly cast off the slavish formulas of conventional style while repudiating the charlatanries that might have replaced old abuses with new.

Throughout the several years that this campaign for romanticism lasted, so to speak, with experiments that were master strokes, Chopin remained firm in both his predilections and aversions. He had absolutely no traffic with those who, in his view, did not sufficiently represent progress and who did not demonstrate a sincere devotion to this progress without thought of exploiting art for professional profit and without chasing after transient effect or success won by the amazement of listeners. He broke the ties that he had openly made when he sensed their annoying restrictions and felt moored too close to shore by bonds that he sensed as rotted. Conversely, he stubbornly refused to form associations with young artists whose success, in his opinion exaggerated, was overmagnified by a modicum of merit. He brought not the slightest praise to what he did not believe was an effectual conquest for art or a serious concept of an artist's task. He wanted no one to laud him by contrivance or concession such as various schools practice in the person of their heads—for these schools have injected (amidst rivalries and encroachments, retreats and invasions of different styles in the different branches of art) negotiations and agreements and pacts similar to those forming the end and means of diplomacy, as well as the cunning and a certain lack of scruple inseparable therefrom. Refusing to support his works by any outside aid in order to force a welcome, he said often enough that he trusted in their beauty to make them appreciated, and he exerted no effort to hasten or facilitate their immediate acceptance.

Chopin gave to our trials and struggles of the time, so filled with uncertainty and still encountering more *dubiously nodding sages* than glorious adversaries, the support of a calm and firm conviction, of a steadiness of character equal to the test of weariness and deceit, of a rare fixity of will; and he also supplied the useful assistance of valuable works which the cause could appropriate. He accompanied his boldnesses with so much charm, proportion, and learning that he was justified in believing in his own genius, so readily did it win admiration. The solid studies he had made, the reflective habits of his youth, the worship of classical beauty in which he was raised forbade his dissipating energy in unhappy gropings and half-successes, as has happened to more than one champion of new ideas. His thoughtful patience in fashioning and finishing his works sheltered him from the critics who fan dissension by seizing upon easy and meaningless victories springing from omissions and careless negligence. Trained early by rigorous rules, even producing beautiful works in which they were adhered to, he ignored them only after proper and sound reflection. He constantly forged ahead by virtue of his principles, free of exaggeration and the pitfall of compromise, and gladly foregoing theoretical formulas in order to pursue only their results. He was less concerned with academic disputes and terminology than with obtaining the best of arguments: a finished work—and so he had the good fortune to avoid personal enmities and troublesome settlements.

Along with a more modern, more simple, and less intense approach, Chopin accorded to art the same reverent worship as the early medieval masters. For him as for them art was a high and holy calling. Like them he was proud of being summoned, and he brought to it religious fervor. This feeling was revealed at the hour of his death by a detail the significance of which is explained more fully by Polish custom. Following a usage that still exists there, though less practiced today, dying persons often choose the garments in which they wished to be buried and which some prepared long in advance.[3] Their most precious and most intimate thoughts were thus expressed or betrayed for the last time. Monastic robes were often selected by

3. The author of *Julie et Adolphe* (a novel modeled after *La nouvelle Héloïse* and very popular at the time of its publication), General K——, was more than eighty years old and still living in a region under the government of Volhynia at the time of our visit to those parts. Conforming to the custom we have mentioned, he had ordered his coffin built, and after thirty years it was still waiting beside his chamber door.

worldly persons; men would request or would refuse the costume of their official labors, according to the memories, glorious or bitter, clinging thereto. Chopin, who among the foremost contemporary artists gave the fewest concerts —Chopin, however, wished to be placed in the grave wearing the garb he had played in.[4] An instinctive and deep feeling, flowing from an inexhaustible fount of enthusiasm for his art, doubtless dictated this final wish as he scrupulously fulfilled the final duties of a Christian and left behind all things earthly, unable to transport aught toward heaven. Long before the approach of death he had linked his love and faith in art to immortality, and he reclined in the coffin, testifying once more and characteristically by a silent symbol to a conviction that he had sustained unbroken throughout his life. He died faithful to himself, adoring the mystical grandeurs of art and its most mystical revelations.

While withdrawing from the whirl of society, as we have said, Chopin focused his tenderness and affection within the radius of family and youthful acquaintances. He preserved constant and frequent relations with them, and he maintained them with exceeding care. His sister Louise was especially dear to him, and a certain similarity in the nature of their minds and the cast of their feelings bound them still more closely together. She journeyed several times from Warsaw to Paris to see him, and finally she

4. This is not the only passage supporting the belief that Liszt received no reply to the questionnaire sent to Chopin's sister.—*Trans.*

came to Paris for the last three months of her brother's life, surrounding him with her devoted attention.

Chopin maintained a regular correspondence with his family, but only with them. One of his peculiarities consisted of not writing letters to others, and it might have been thought that he had vowed never to send any to strangers. It was curious to see him resort to all expedients to escape the necessity of scribbling the most insignificant note. Many a time he preferred to cross Paris, from one end to the other, to decline a dinner or to share some slight information, rather than spare himself this trouble by writing a few lines. To most of his friends his handwriting was practically unknown. It is said that he departed from this habit in favor of his lovely countrywomen, some of whom hold several notes in his hand, written in Polish. This breach of what could have been taken as a law with him is explainable by the pleasure he had in speaking that language. He used it by choice with his family and was happy in translating its most expressive phrases. He was highly skilled in French, as Slavs generally are, and because of his French origin it had been taught to him with special care. But he was prejudiced against it and criticized it for being displeasing to the ear and cold in essence. This manner of judging it is quite prevalent among the Poles. They use it with great facility, speak it commonly among themselves (often better than their own tongue), but then complain to those unfamiliar with Polish that they cannot express the ethereal nuances and shimmerings of thought in an idiom different from theirs. It is sometimes majesty, sometimes passion and sometimes gracefulness which, in their opinion, are lacking in the French language. If they are asked the meaning of a verse or a word quoted in Polish, the immediate reply to the foreigner is inevitably: *Oh! that is untranslatable!* Then come the remarks that are especially designed to explain the explanation and to show all the subtleties and implications and contrasts embedded in those *untranslatable* words! We have mentioned several examples, and these, joined to others, lead us to believe that this language has the advantage of conceptualizing abstract nouns and that, as it developed, it drew upon the nation's poetic genius to establish a striking and exact relationship between ideas by means of etymologies, derivations, and synonyms. The result is like a colored reflection, dark or bright, cast upon all expressions which, in a manner of speaking, stimulate the mind to hear the corresponding sound of a shifting third that readily plunges the thought into a major or minor strain. The wealth of the language always permits the choice of mode, but this wealth can pose a difficulty. Perhaps the use of foreign languages, which are so prevalent in Poland, may be attributed to the indolence of mind and effort that seeks to escape the fatigue of skilled discourse. And this is indispensable in a language filled with sudden depths and with brevities so emphatic that banality becomes intolerable and approximations awkward. The vague agreements of ill-defined thoughts cannot be compressed in the sturdy structure of its grammar; the idea cannot emerge from a strangely barren starkness as long as it remains within the limits of the commonplace, and beyond that it demands a rare precision of phrase not to become baroque. Because of this characteristic of the language, perhaps, the literature of this land shows a greater number of masterpieces, in proportion to its authors, than elsewhere. He who ventures to use the language feels himself a master.

[The language cannot be reproached for wanting in harmony or lacking in musical charm. The frequency of consonants is not always and absolutely responsible for the harshness of a language, but rather the way they are associated. It might be said that some have a dull and cold color only through the absence of well-defined and strongly marked sounds. The frequent repetition of certain consonants shades and rhythms the language and gives it strength, the preponderance of vowels producing only a kind of clear, pale tinge that must be relieved by darker hues. Our manner of hearing is painfully injured by the clashing, rough, and discordant encounters of incongruous consonants. Slavic languages, it is true, employ many consonants, but generally with relationships in sound that sometimes flatter the ear and are almost never completely dissonant, even when they are more striking than pleasant. The quality of their sounds is full, rich, and of many shades. They are not compressed into a kind of narrow ambiance, but extend to a range that is considerable through the variety of intonations, now low and again high. There is nothing dry in the sound of the Slavic *l*, well-nigh impossible to pronounce by those who did not learn it in childhood. It strikes the ear with an impression similar to the touch of thick woolen velvet, rough and pliant at the same time. Since the union of choppy consonances is rare and assonances abound, this comparison might be applied to the total effect which foreigners receive from idiomatic speech. In Polish there are many words that imitate the sound of objects designated. The reiterated repetitions of *ch* (*h* aspirate), of *sz* (*ch* in French), of *rz*, of *cz*, so frightening to the uninitiated eye but with little of the barbaric in their sound (they are pronounced almost exactly like *geai* and *tche* [in French]), facilitate the meaning through sound. The word *dzwiek* (read *dzwïinque*), meaning sound, offers a quite characteristic example; it would seem difficult to reproduce better the sensation felt by the ear in experiencing a tuning-fork's resonance. Among the consonants gathered in groups that produce greatly varied sounds, now metallic and again buzzing, hissing or growling, there are mingled numerous diphthongs and vowels which often become somewhat nasal, *a* and *e* being pronounced like *on* and *in* [in French] when a cedilla is attached. Alongside the *c* (*tse* [in French]), spoken with great softness, sometimes *ć* (*tsie* [in French]), the accented *s* is almost chirped. The *z* has three sounds, actually a chord: *ż* (jais [in French]), *z* (*zed* [in French]), and *z* (*zied* [in French]). The *y* is a vowel of muffled tone which we could no more reproduce in French than *l*, but which similarly gives the language an indescribable glow. These fine and delicate elements enable the women to adopt a lingering and singing accent, which they usually carry over into other languages, and to turn into kinds of recitatives and improvised threnodies when the topics of conversation are serious and sad, all the while using a strange enunciation and a rather childish lisp. They interpolate short, pearly laughter, little cries of interruption, brief prolongings of high notes from which they quickly drop by an indefinable series of chromatic half- and quarter-tones to pause upon a low note; thence they go to modulations that are innumerable and fleeting and original, and bewilder the ear unaccustomed to this lovely warbling, imbued with that deceptive air of irony and sly mockery that is peculiar to the song of certain birds. They like to twitter, and piquant intervals, unexpected breaks, and delightful shadings appear quite naturally in this dainty chatter, which makes the language as spoken by women sound much gentler and more caressing than when spoken by men. The latter, when stirred to speak it elegantly, give it a masculine tone which seems strongly congenial to the promotion of eloquence, once so cultivated in Poland. In these rich and varied materials poetry finds a diversity of rhythms, of prosody, of rhyme, and an abundance of assonance which enables it to follow musically, after a fashion, the shades of the feelings and scenes that it depicts, not only in short onomatopoeia but throughout long declamations. The resemblance between Polish and Russian has rightly been compared to that between Latin and Italian. The Russian language is, indeed, more flowing, more languid, more lulling, more yearning. Its rhythm is especially suitable for singing, and the exquisite poems, those of Zukowski and Pushkin, seem to contain a melody fully sketched out by the meter of the verses; certain stanzas (*Le Châle noir, Le Talisman*), for example, appear ready to release an *arioso* or a sweet *cantabile*. Ancient Slavonic, the language of the Eastern Church, has a noble majesty. More guttural than other idioms that derive from it, it is grandly severe and monotone like the Byzantine paintings preserved in the worship that it serves. It possesses the aspect of a holy tongue ministering to a single sentiment, and it has not been changed or fashioned by secular urge.][5]

In dealings with his parents Chopin exhibited a delightful graciousness. Not satisfied by confining his entire correspondence to them, he took advantage of his stay in Paris to obtain for them the thousand surprises inherent in novelties, bagatelles, and knickknacks as pretty as they were trifling. Their charm was in their freshness. He sought for everything that he believed would be welcome in Warsaw, and supplemented his letters with a ceaseless flow of presents. He wanted these objects to be preserved so as to be always among those for whom they were intended. For his part he set great price on all the proofs of their affection. Receiving news from them or evidence of their remembrance was a festive occasion for him; he shared it with no one, but the care he lavished on all the things they sent was noticeable. The least of them was precious to him, and he not only forbade others to use them—he was visibly upset if anyone touched them.

Material elegance was as natural to him as mental,

5. This long interpolation appears as a footnote in the first and second French editions.—*Trans.*

and was as obvious in his belongings as in his distinguished manners. He dearly loved flowers. Without rivaling the glittering richness in which certain famous women of Paris were then decorating their apartments, he knew how to maintain, here as in his dress, the balance between too much and too little, the instinctive line of *perfect propriety*.

Keeping free of others in time, thought, and action, he often preferred the company of women, since it involved him less in subsequent relations. He would gladly spend whole evenings playing blindman's buff with young folks, telling them little stories that made them laugh, the rippling laughter of youth, sweeter than the nightingale's song. He enjoyed the country and life in a château. He was ingenious in varying its pleasures and in increasing its cheering events. Moreover, he liked to work there, and several of his best compositions, written at such moments, perhaps hold the memory of his happiest days.

6

YOUTH, NATIONALISM, AND
MUSICAL SYMPATHIES

*C*HOPIN WAS BORN in 1810 in Zelazowa-Wola, near Warsaw. By a chance that rarely falls to children it seems that in his early years he kept no memory of his age, and the date of his birth was fixed in his mind only by a watch that Mme Catalani gave him in 1820. It bore this inscription: *Madame Catalani, à Frédéric Chopin, âgé de dix ans.* Perhaps the artist's presentiment gave the child a foreglimpse of his future! But there was nothing remarkable in the course of his boyhood; it probably unfolded calmly and showed few special developments. As he was frail and sickly, his family's attention was centered on his health. From that time, unquestionably, he acquired his friendly manner, his open charm, his silence in suffering, all born from the desire of allaying the fears he was causing. In those early years no precociousness of ability and no advance sign of a remarkable flowering pointed to any future superiority of soul or mind or talent. The little fellow was seen to smile and suffer, he was always patient and cheerful, and he so gladdened his watchers by becoming neither moody nor morose that they were doubtless happy to cherish these qualities, believing that he opened his heart without reserve and surrendered the secret of all his thoughts. But there are souls who, at the beginning of life, are like rich travelers thrown by fate amidst simple herdsmen who heap gifts upon them during their stay—not proportionate to their wealth, but sufficient nevertheless to astonish their hosts and to spread happiness deep in their simple existence. These souls give as much, and more, in affectionate outpourings as those who surround them. The recipient is satisfied, and generosity is taken for granted, but in truth these souls have poured out little and have lavished but few of their treasures.

The environment that Chopin knew from the very beginning, and in which he grew up (as in a soft and solid cradle), was calm, consistent, and industrious, and it offered him always the dearest and sweetest models of simplicity and devoutness and honor. Domestic virtues and religious habits, pious charity and ingrained modesty bathed him in a purified atmosphere from which his imagination drew that velvety softness of plants that are never exposed to the grime of the highway.

He received instruction in music at an early age, beginning to learn it when he was nine. Soon he was put in the hands of Ziwna [Zywny], a devout disciple of Sebastian

Bach, who guided his studies for many years in the line of strictest classicism. It must not be assumed that, when he adopted the career of musician, the glamor of easy fame or any fantastic vista dazzled his eyes and the hopes of his family. He was made to study seriously and conscientiously in order one day to become a skilled and knowledgeable master, with no undue thought of renown that might come as the fruit of lessons and dutiful labor.

Still quite youthful, he was placed in one of Warsaw's leading schools, thanks to the generous and percipient protection which Prince Antoine Radziwill consistently granted to all the arts and to young talents whose capacity he recognized as a distinguished man and artist. Prince Radziwill was not a mere dilettante in music—he was a remarkable composer. His fine score of *Faust*, published some years ago and performed at regular intervals by the *Singakademie* in Berlin, seems to us, through its intimate penetration into the poem's essence, far superior to other attempts to transfer it to the realm of music. By augmenting the very restricted means of Chopin's family, the Prince presented to the boy the priceless gift of a thorough education, and no part of it was neglected. From his entry into college to the final completion of his studies, it was always the Prince (his enlightened mind understanding the demands of an artist's career) who supported the boy through the mediation of a friend, M. Antoine Korzuchowski; and the latter, ever since that time, maintained a constant companionship with Chopin until the composer's final days.

In speaking of this period of his life, we are pleased to quote some charming lines more justly applicable to him than other pages where his likeness was believed perceptible but where we could find it only in the distortion resulting from a silhouette drawn on a stretchable fabric and pulled askew in opposite directions.

Gentle, sensitive and exquisite in all things, he had at fifteen years of age all the graces of youth joined to the seriousness of maturity. He remained delicate of body as of mind. But this lack of muscular development meant the retaining of a beauty, an exceptional countenance, that was, so to speak, both ageless and sexless. It was not the bold and masculine appearance of a descendant of that race of ancient magnates who could only drink and hunt and war; neither was it the effeminate sweetness of a rosy cherub. It was something like those idealized creatures that medieval poetry called upon to serve for the adornment of Christian temples. An angel beautiful of face like a sadly noble woman, of pure and slender form like a young god of Olympus, and expression both tender and severe, both chaste and impassioned.

That was the substance of his being. Nothing was purer and, at the same time, more exalted than his thoughts, nothing more constant, more concentrated and more completely devoted than his affections. . . . But this being understood only what was indistinguishable from himself . . . all the rest existed for him only as a kind of vexing dream which he tried to escape from while living in the midst of society. Always lost in his trances, he disliked reality. As a child he could not touch a sharp instrument without being wounded; as an adult he could not face a man different from himself without colliding against this living contradiction. . . . What saved him from perpetual antagonism was a voluntary and soon inveterate habit of seeing and hearing nothing that generally displeased him, unless it touched his personal affections. Persons who did not think as he did became like phantoms in his eyes, and, since he was charmingly polite, his courteous benevolence could hide what was only a cold disdain, even an unconquerable aversion. . . .

He never had an hour of expansiveness without paying for it by several hours of withdrawal. The moral causes for this might have been too slight and too subtle to be glimpsed by the naked eye. A microscope would have been needed to read in his soul where so little of the light of the living ever pierced. . . .

It is remarkably strange that, with such a character, he could find any friends. And yet he did have some, not only his mother's, who esteemed him as the worthy son of a noble woman, but also young people of his own age who loved him warmly and were loved by him. . . . He had a high conception of friendship and, in the period of first illusions, he willingly believed that he and his friends, raised in nearly the same manner and on the same principles, would never change opinions and would reach no essential disagreement.

Outwardly he was so affectionate, as a consequence of his fine education and natural grace, that he had the gift of pleasing even those who did not know him. His lovely face spoke in his favor, his physical frailty made him interesting in the eyes of women. The full and flowing culture of his mind, the sweet and pleasant freshness of his words won him the attention of enlightened men. As for those of a coarser mold, they liked his exquisite courtesy, and with their open geniality they responded to it the more since they failed to realize that it was the exercise of a duty with sympathy playing no part.

If these persons could have probed his nature, they would have said he was more friendly than loving, and as far as they were concerned, this would have been true. But how could they have guessed this when his very few attachments were so vital, so deep, and so constant? . . .

In ordinary life, association with him was delightful. He practiced all forms of kindness with uncommon graciousness, and in expressing his gratitude he displayed a deep emotion that paid for friendship on usurious terms.

Each day he was prone to believe he was dying, and in this thought he accepted the cares of a friend, concealing from him, however, the shortness of time that he could enjoy his solicitude. He had a great outward courage, and if he did not entertain the thought of approaching death with the heroic jauntiness of youth, at least he savored its expectation with a kind of bitter sensuality.[1]

It was in this early period of his youth that he felt affection for a girl whose deep feeling of reverent homage never ceased to follow him. The tempest that snatched Chopin up in one of its blasts and tore him far from his native land, like a bewildered and distraught bird surprised on the branch of a foreign tree, shattered this first love and deprived the exile of both a country and a devoted and faithful wife. In meeting the glory perhaps not yet thought of, he met no more the happiness he had dreamed of with her. She was beautiful and sweet, this young girl, like one of Luini's madonnas, her glances laden with sober tenderness. She remained calm and sad, and the sadness surely swelled in that pure soul when she realized that no devo-

1. The second edition, but not the first, identified this quotation as coming from George Sand's *Lucrezia Floriani* (1847). —*Trans.*

tion like hers softened the existence of him whom she would have adored with artless submission, exclusive devotion, and that innocent and sublime abandon that transforms woman into angel.

Those whom nature overwhelms with the fatal, beautiful gifts of genius are forbidden to neglect the care of their glory for that of their love. They probably have the right to impose limits on the sacrifice of their personality.

But it may be that divine emotions springing from complete devotion will be regretted even in the presence of genius' most brilliant endowments; for that artless submission and love's abandon, which submerge the woman and her being and her will and her name into those of the man she loves, can alone lead the man to think, when he leaves this life, that he has shared it with her, that his love has brought her what no chance lover or friend would have yielded her: the honor of his name and the peace of his heart.

Suddenly separated from Chopin, this girl was faithful to his memory, and to all that he left behind. She bestowed her filial affection upon his parents, and Chopin's father never wanted the portrait she had drawn of him (in days when hope was alive) replaced in his home by another, even should it come from a more experienced brush. Many years after, we saw the pale cheeks of this sorrowful woman slowly color, as alabaster blushes before an unveiled light, when she looked at this portrait and her eyes met the eyes of the father.

The charming, easygoing nature that Chopin brought

to the schoolroom at once gained the love of his companions, especially of Prince Borys Czetwertynski and his brothers. When holidays and vacations arrived, he would often go to spend them with these boys and their mother, Princess Louise Czetwertynska, who cultivated music with a true appreciation of its beauties and was soon able to discover the poet in the musician. She was the first, perhaps, who made Chopin realize the delight in being understood as well as heard. The Princess was still beautiful and had a sympathetic mind enhanced by noble qualities. Her salon was one of the most brilliant and select in Warsaw. There Chopin often met the most distinguished women of this capital. There he knew those fascinating beauties, whose fame was European, at a time when Warsaw was renowned for the brilliance and elegance and charm of its society. Through the mediation of the Princess he had the honor of being presented at the home of Princess de Lowicz, and here he was brought together with Countess Zamoyska, Princess Radziwill, Princess Thérèse Jablonowska, enchantresses all, surrounded by so many other beauties less illustrious.

It was his lot, while still young, to play the piano for their dancing. At these parties, which might have been called fairy gatherings, he was able to discover, many times perhaps, the secrets of excited and tender hearts fleetingly disclosed in the whirling rounds. He could easily read those souls who were drawn to his youth by affection and friendship, and he could easily learn the formula of his country's poetic ideal: leaven and cream of roses, gunpowder, and angels' tears. When his wandering fingers caressed the keys and unexpectedly struck some meaningful chords, he could glimpse the flow of furtive tears on the cheeks of love-smitten girls and neglected women, could see the moistened eyes of young men, passionate and jealous of glory. Did no lovely maiden, asking for a simple *prélude*, place her exquisite arm on his piano to support her dreaming head and let him sense in her glance the song her heart was singing? Did no group, like frolicking nymphs, to wheedle some waltz of dizzying speed, shower him with smiles which taught him to merge with their merriment? He saw unfolded there, in the mazurka, the decorous grace of his magnificent countrywomen, and he retained an imperishable memory of the glamor of their allure and their restraint.

Sometimes, apparently casual but with that involuntary and quiet emotion that accompanies thoughts of our early pleasures, he would say that he first understood all the feeling that the airs and rhythms of national dances could hold and express on those days when he saw the lovely fairies at some grand and magical fête, dazzlingly adorned and bedecked, and practicing coquetries in a way that kindles all hearts. They quicken love, and also blind it and discourage it. The muslins of India, which the Greeks even said were woven of air, gave way to sumptuous Venetian velvets; perfumed roses and colorful camellias from the conservatory yielded to proudly flowered jewel caskets—then it seemed to Chopin that, however perfect the orchestra might sound, the women skimmed less swiftly over the floor, their laughter was less ringing, their eyes sparkled less radiantly, and fatigue was felt sooner than on those evenings when the dance had been improvised because he had suddenly electrified all hearers. If he electrified them, it was because he could reproduce in hieroglyphic tones, though easily grasped by the initiated, what his ear had caught of the hushed and passionate whisperings of the heart, comparable to the fraxinella, that vigorous plant with flowers always wrapped in a vapor as imperceptible as it is inflammable. He had seen the glimmer of illusory phantoms and celestial visions in this highly rarefied air. He had sensed the swarm of emotions ever rumbling there, how these emotions flit through the soul, and how ready they always are to jostle and impose and upset, although their agitation and pulsation at no time disturb the beautiful harmony of visible grace. Thus did Chopin learn to relish and hold in high esteem noble and proportioned manners—when they are joined to an emotional sensitivity that saves refinement from dullness, wards off the anticipation of bitterness, prevents conformity from becoming tyrannous (and good taste from becoming rigid), and allows no feelings to resemble, as often happens elsewhere, that stony, calcareous vegetation, hard and brittle, that is sadly called flowers of iron: *flos ferri*.

These first glimpses of a world where the rule of formality fails to hide hardenings of the heart led Chopin to believe that conformity and decorum, instead of being a covering mask veiling each individual's character beneath symmetrical patterns, served only to subdue the passions

without stifling them. They remove perverting uncouth-
ness, debasing realism of expression, vulgarizing indifference, palling vehemence and fatiguing exuberance. And
they teach *the lovers of the unattainable* to strive to join
all the virtues revealed by a knowledge of evil to all the
virtues that cause *it to be forgotten in addressing the object
of love.*[2] These early visions of his youth, as they took root
in the perspective of memory, increased for him in charm
and enchantment and glamor. They fascinated him all the
more since no opposing reality could destroy and contradict
that fascination secretly secluded in a corner of his memory
and imagination. And they made all the more invincible
his repugnance for that freedom of action, that brutish
command of caprice, that determination to drink to the
dregs the cup of fantasy, that stormy pursuit of all of
life's chances and disparities which are encountered in that
queer and never-quiet circle known as Bohemia.

Many a time has a poet or an artist appeared who
embodies in himself a people and a period, and he une-
quivocally represents in his creations the types they strive
for and would like to realize. Chopin was this poet for his
land and for the period that saw his birth. He embodied
in his imagination, he represented through his genius the
poetic feeling then most widespread and most deeply im-
planted in his country. Poland had many singers—and she
possesses some who take rank and place among the foremost poets of the world. More than ever her writers endeavor to bring out the most noteworthy and most glori-

2. *Lucrezia Floriani.* Identified in the 2nd edition.—*Trans.*

ous aspects of her history and her spirit, the most striking and picturesque aspects of her land and her customs. But Chopin differed from them by forming no preconceived plan, and he surpassed them perhaps in originality. He did not want to seek for this result. His creation of the ideal was not *a priori*. He recollected patriotic glories with no determination to live in the past; he understood and sang of contemporary love and tears without advance analysis. He neither studied nor contrived to be a national musician, and he may have been astonished to hear himself so called. Like true national poets, he sang without fixed plan, without predetermined choice, whatever inspiration most spontaneously dictated. And in this way, easily and effortlessly, the most idealized form of emotion appeared in his songs, feelings which had quickened his childhood and embellished his youth. In this way, too, the ideal was released from his pen, the ideal that is real and truly existing for his people, so to speak, since every one in general and each one in particular approaches it by one path or another. Without special intent he collected in luminous sheaves impressions which were confusedly felt throughout his country. They were fragmentedly lodged in all hearts and vaguely apprehended by only a few. The reproduction in a poetic formula which attracts the imagination of all nations and catches the blurred outlines of sentiments scattered but often encountered among compatriots—is not the gift of accomplishing this the distinguishing mark of national artists?

Since efforts are now being made, not unreasonably, to

assemble carefully the indigenous melodies of various regions, it would appear to us still more interesting to devote
some attention to the nature which the talent of certain
authors can assume when they are more specially inspired
than others by national genius. Up to the present there
have been few whose notable compositions lie outside of
the great categories of Italian music and German music.
But it is likely that, with the tremendous development
that art seems destined to undergo in our century (perhaps
renewing for us the glorious era of *cinque cento* painters),
authors will arise whose works will bear the stamp of an
originality based on differences of constitution, race, and
climate. It is likely that, in music as in the other arts, the
influence of country upon great masters will be perceptible
and their products marked by the reflection of the peoples'
spirit, more complete, more poetically true, and more interesting to study in the crude, incorrect, groping and quavering sketches of popular inspiration.

Chopin will be ranked in the company of the foremost
musicians who thus individualized in themselves the poetic
sense of a nation, but not only because he chose the rhythm
of *Polonaises*, *Mazurkas*, and *Cracoviennes* and called
many of his compositions by such names. Had he limited
himself to multiplying them, he would only have constantly
reproduced the same pattern and the memory of the same
experience and deed, a reproduction that would soon have
been tedious, serving merely to prolong a form quickly
become more or less boring. If his name stands for a poet
who is essentially Polish, it is because he used this form

solely to express a manner of feeling more prevalent in his country than elsewhere and because the expression of the same emotions occurs in all the forms that he selected. His *Préludes,* and *Études,* his *Nocturnes* above all, his *Scherzos* and *Concertos,* his shortest compositions as well as the most extended breathe the same type of sensibility expressed in varying degrees, modified and varied in a thousand ways, but always one and unchanging. An eminently subjective composer, Chopin gave to all his works the same vital spark, and he inspirited all of his creations by his own life. Thus all of his works are bound together by a unity, whence it happens that their beauties, like their defects, are always the result of the same order of emotion and a single manner of feeling, a poet's basic requirement for his songs to stir all the hearts of his country to tremble in unison.

We should have liked to explain here, by analogous word and picture, the impressions corresponding to that sensibility, exquisite yet irritable, which is peculiar to ardent, inconstant hearts and to haughty and deeply wounded natures. We do not flatter ourselves that we have succeeded in capturing much of the ethereal and fragrant flame in the narrow stricture of words, could this even be accomplished. Do not words always seem weak, paltry, cold, and dry after the strong and sweet excitement that other arts can provide, and is it not rightly said *that of all ways to express a sentiment, words are the most inadequate?* We do not flatter ourselves that we have been able, in these lines, to achieve that delicate stroke of brush needed to retrace what Chopin depicted with such inimitable lightness of hand, for there everything is rarefied, even to the source of anger and rage. There the frank and simple and impulsive promptings disappear. Before birth they have all passed through the sieve of a fertile, ingenious, and exacting imagination, and it has entangled them and affected their flow. They all demand insight to be grasped and delicacy to be described. In grasping them and describing them with infinite art and extraordinarily fine discrimination, Chopin became an artist of the first rank. And so it is only by long and patient study, by constant pursuit of his thought through its manifold ramifications that full understanding and sufficient admiration are gained. Then it becomes clear with what genius he made his thought evident and tangible, never letting it flag or stagnate.

He was so thoroughly and uniquely filled with sentiments, the most cherished types of which he believed he knew in his youth—with the only sentiments he wished to express in art—and he held for art such a singular, unchanging view that his artistic inclinations could not fail to be affected thereby. He sought in the grand examples and masterpieces of art only what corresponded to his own nature. He was pleased by what was sympathetic; he scarcely rendered justice to what was distant. Combining and dreaming of the often opposed qualities of passion and grace, he exercised a great firmness of judgment and avoided any mean partiality, but he barely paused before the finest beauty and most wondrous skill when they offended any facet of his poetic conception. Whatever admiration he entertained for Beethoven's works, certain portions seemed to him too roughly hewn. Their structure was too robust to please him; he deemed their rages too roaring, he felt their passion approached disaster. The leonine quality found in each figure of his phrases was too substantial for Chopin, and the seraphic and Raphaelesque outlines appearing in the midst of this genius' powerful creations became for him at times almost painful in their cutting contrast.

In spite of the charm he acknowledged in some of Schubert's melodies, he listened unwillingly to those with a shape too angular for his ear, where feeling is stripped bare, where, as it were, the trembling of flesh and the cracking of bones become perceptible in sorrow's embrace. All the fierce harshness repelled him. In music, as in literature and in the ways of life, everything verging on melodrama was torture to him. He was repelled by the furious and frenzied face of romanticism; he could not endure the confused effects and excesses of delirium. "Except for strict reservations he did not like Shakespeare. He found his characters too closely patterned from life and speaking too realistically. He preferred epic and lyrical fusions which cast a shade over the pitiful details of humanity. For this reason he spoke little and rarely listened. He wanted to form his own thoughts or accept those of others only when they had attained a certain loftiness."[3]

That nature, so constantly self-governed, so filled with sensitive reserve, to which divination and premonition and

3. *Lucrezia Floriani*. Identified in the 2nd edition.—*Trans.*

the half-seen offered the charm of suggestion so cherished by poets who know the aim of unfinished words and incomplete ideas—that nature could only experience vexation, like a shock, from the effrontery that leaves nothing to be sensed and nothing to be grasped beyond the obvious. Had he been forced to express his views in this respect, we believe he would have admitted that his taste allowed him to express feelings only when the greater share remained to be apprehended. If what is commonly called the *classical* in art seemed to impose on him too-methodical restrictions, if he refused to be bound by these manacles and to be frozen by conventional system, if he fought against the confines of a square cage, the reason was that he must ascend into the clouds, sing like a lark in the blue of heaven, never to drop from those heights, and to relax only in soaring in those lofty regions—like the bird of paradise which, it was formerly said, only tasted sleep with wings widespread, lulled by the breath of space high in the air where it rested from flight. But he quite as stubbornly refused to plunge into forest lairs to sample their many howlings and wailings, nor would he venture into the fearful deserts and trace paths which the treacherous wind mockingly sweeps away as the bold adventurer endeavors to make them.

Everything in Italian music that is simple, glittering, and devoid of ornament as of skill; everything in German music that is stamped with vulgar, though powerful, energy displeased him equally. With reference to Schubert he said one day "the sublime becomes drab when followed by the common or the trivial." Among composers for the piano,

Hummel was the one whom he read again and again with intense pleasure, and in his eyes Mozart was the ideal type, the poet supreme, for more rarely than any other would he deign to cross the step separating the distinctive from the commonplace. He loved exactly that in Mozart which earned the latter a reproach from his father, who said after witnessing a performance of *Idomeneo:* "You were wrong to put in nothing for the dolts." Papageno's gaiety stimulated Chopin's; Tamino's love and his mysterious ordeals seemed worthy of Mozart's attention; Zerlina and Masetto amused by their refined ingenuousness; he understood Donna Anna's vengeance because it only cloaked her mourning more securely. And yet his straining after purity, his abhorrence of what was common were such that even in *Don Juan,* even in this immortal masterpiece he discovered passages which, in our hearing, he regretted. This saddened, without lessening, his adoration for Mozart. He succeeded in forgetting what repelled him, but to become reconciled with it was impossible. Was he not governed here by the grievous quality of instinctive, irrational, and unyielding superiority which no persuasion, demonstration, or effort can bring to a point of even being indifferent toward objects of such antipathetic appearance and such insurmountable aversion that a kind of phobia results?

When his school years were over and he had completed the study of harmony with Professor Joseph Elsner, who taught him the most difficult and least-known things —to be exacting with himself and to realize the advantages gained only from patience and industry—his parents wanted him to travel in order to hear fine performances of great works. For this purpose he enjoyed brief stays in several German cities. In 1830 he had left Warsaw for one of these short excursions when the revolution of November 29 broke out.

Forced to remain in Vienna, he was heard there in a few concerts, but during that winter the Viennese public, usually so intelligent, so responsive to all shades of performance and all subtleties of thought, was inattentive. The young artist failed to produce quite the sensation he had a right to expect. He left Vienna intending to go to London, but first he came to Paris, where he planned to stop only briefly. Added to his passport, stamped for England, were the words *passing through Paris*. This phrase settled his future. Long years after, when he seemed more than acclimated and naturalized in France, he would still laughingly say: "I am only passing through."

Upon reaching Paris he gave several concerts, at once winning the deep admiration of high society and of young artists. We remember his first appearance in the rooms of Pleyel, where we were so delighted that the most vociferous applause seemed insufficient for the talent that was opening a new phase of poetic sentiment and presenting happy innovations in the substance of his art.

Contrary to most of the young newcomers, he was not confused for a moment by the dazzlement or intoxication of the triumph. He accepted it without pride and without false modesty, he felt no pricks of a puerile vanity exhibited by successful upstarts. All his countrymen in

Paris at the time extended the most eager and affectionate welcome. As an intimate he often visited the homes of Prince Czartoryski, Countess Plater, Mme de Komar, and her daughters Princess de Beauveau and Countess Delphine Potocka. The beauty and indescribable, spiritual grace of the last-named made her one of the most admired types of society queens. He dedicated to her his second *Concerto*, which contains the *adagio* we mentioned elsewhere. The ethereal beauty of the Countess, her talent, and her enchanting voice captivated him and exerted the most admiring fascination. This voice was destined to be the last to resound in his ear and to blend in his mind the sweetest tones of earth with the welcoming chords of angels.

He saw many young Poles: Fontana; Orda, who seemed destined to a promising future and was killed in Algeria at twenty years of age; Counts Plater, Grzymala, Ostrowski, and Szembeck; Prince Casimir Lubomirski; and others. Polish families subsequently coming to Paris were eager to know him, and by preference he regularly associated with a group predominantly consisting of his compatriots. Through them he remained informed about all that was happening in his country and in addition maintained a kind of musical correspondence therewith. He enjoyed receiving airs and new songs that visitors from Poland brought to Paris, and when he liked the words of these tunes he would often add a melody to them which quickly became popular in his country without the composer's name ever being known. As a number of these musical thoughts, solely inspired by the heart, grew considerable, Chopin, in his last days, was of a mind to assemble them for publication. But he no longer had leisure to do this, and they are lost and scattered like the fragrance of flowers that grow in deserted places some day to scent the path of the unknown traveler that chance brings by. In Poland we have heard some of the melodies attributed to him and truly worthy of his hand, but who today would dare to make an unsure sorting of the poet's inspiration and that of his people?

For a long time Chopin held aloof from the most sought-after celebrities in Paris. Their noisy following disturbed him. He on his side aroused less curiosity than they, for his character and customs had more genuine originality than apparent eccentricity. And he had stinging replies for those who incautiously attempted to exploit his ability. One day, after he had left the dining room, an ill-advised host, who had innocently hoped and promised to give his guests, like a rare dessert, some piece played by Chopin, pointed to an open piano. He realized that he who reckons without the host must reckon twice. At first he simply declined, but wearied finally by a too-importunate persistence he said, his voice muffled as if to lend sharpness to his words: "Ah, monsieur, I have barely dined."

7

LELIA (GEORGE SAND)
AND IDEALISM

*I*N 1836 Mme Sand had published not only *Indiana, Valentine,* and *Jacques,* but also *Lélia,*[1] that poem about which she later remarked: "If I regret having written it, the reason is that I can do it no more. If I returned to a similar state of mind, I should be greatly solaced by being able to begin it again."[2] And indeed, the novel's water-color tints must have seemed pallid to Mme Sand after she had wielded the sculptor's chisel and hammer in cutting that huge statue, in molding those sweeping lines and reliefs, those sinuous muscles, which retain a bewildering attractiveness in their monumental fixity. Under long contemplation they move us grievously as if, contrary to Pygmalion's miracle, some living Galatea is before us—abundantly alive,

1. 1832, 1832, 1834, and 1833, respectively.—*Trans.*
2. *Lettres d'un voyageur* [1834].

sensually aquiver, and vitalized by the tenderness which the loving artist would have infused into the stone, stifling its breath and congealing its blood with the hope of augmenting and immortalizing its beauty. Thus is nature transformed into a work of art, but it is sad to understand how love can shift into admiration instead of admiration increasing through love.

Dark and olive-hued Lélia! thou hast trod in lonely ways, depressed like Lara, shaken like Manfred, rebellious like Cain, but fiercer, more pitiless, more comfortless than they, for no man's heart has been found feminine enough to love thee as they were loved, to pay thine assertive charms the homage of blind and implicit submission, of silent and deep devotion, to shelter its obedience beneath thine amazonian strength! Woman-hero like unto those woman warriors, thou hast been valiant and eager for combat, like them thou hast not feared to expose the satiny fineness of thy countenance to sun and harsh wind, to harden thy frail limbs by fatigue and so remove the strength of their weakness. Like them thou must needs have donned a cuirass, wounding and tearing, to protect a woman's breast which, as vital as life and as secret as the grave, man adores when his heart is its sole and impenetrable shield!

Blunting her chisel in polishing this image—its haughtiness and condescension, its glance tortured and darkened by the approach of a pure gaze, its locks waving with electric life, reminding us of ancient cameos with magnificent features demanding admiration, a fine and fatal brow and the lordly smile of the Gorgon whose look benumbed and stopped the heart—Mme Sand vainly sought another form for the feeling that gnawed her unsatisfied soul. Having fashioned with infinite art this proud image, which assumed the masculine virtues in place of what she rejected—the supreme virtue of abasement in love, that virtue which the poet of vastest intellect placed at the pinnacle of the empyrean and called "the eternal feminine" [*das ewig Weibliche*], that virtue which is love existing before its joys and surviving all its griefs—having called curses upon Don Juan and having her [*Lélia*] sing a hymn to Desire (and she, like Don Juan, spurning the one sensuality that crowns desire: sacrifice); having avenged Elvina by creating Stenio; having scorned men more than Don Juan had degraded women. Mme Sand portrayed in *Lettres d'un voyageur* that quavering weakness and aching lethargy that seize the artist after he has embodied in a work the emotion that absorbed him. His imagination continues under its dominance, but he discovers no other form for its idealization. This poet's penalty was well understood by Byron who, in recreating Tasso, makes him shed his bitterest tears not over his prison or his chains or his physical sufferings or over man's ignominy, but over his finished epic, over the realm of his thought which, slipping away, makes him aware at last of the frightful realities around him.

One of Chopin's musical friends, among those who had welcomed him to Paris with the greatest joy, often spoke at this time of this truly exceptional artist in Mme

Sand's hearing. She heard praise of his ability and more of his poetic genius; she knew his works and admired their amorous sweetness. She was struck by the abundance of emotion permeating this poetry and by the heartfelt outpourings in a tone so lofty and nobly distinguished. Some of Chopin's countrymen told her about Polish women with the enthusiasm this subject inevitably arouses, augmented further by the recent memory of the sublime sacrifices they had so many times performed during the last war. She heard in their tales and in the poetic inspiration of the Polish artist an ideal of love that assumed the aspect of worship for woman. She believed that here, fully independent and in no way inferior, her rôle was rising to the magical powers of the Peri, that superior intelligence befriending man. She did not sense, perhaps, what a long sequence of suffering and silence, of patience and forbearance, of indulgence and courageous perseverance lay beneath this proud and resigned ideal. It commanded admiration, but was sad to behold. It resembled those plants with rosy corollas, their stems intertwining in a net of long and many strands that breathe life into ruins. Their purpose is to adorn, and Nature makes them grow over the aged mortar disclosed by the tottering stones. In her ingenious and exhaustless munificence she throws these lovely veils over the decay of human handiwork!

This artist did not shape his fancies in porphyry and marble, did not form his creations in massive caryatids that, high-perched, cast their thought downward like the scorching rays of a sun in the zenith, but on the contrary stripped them of all weight, obliterated their outlines and was ready, if need be, to remove the very structure from the ground and hang it in the clouds like the aerial palaces of Fata Morgana. Thus impressed, Mme Sand was perhaps only the more attracted by these forms of intangible lightness toward the ideal that she believed they manifested. Although her arm was strong enough to sculpt in the round, her hand was also delicate enough to trace those barely perceptible reliefs where, on scarcely raised stone, only the shadow of an indelible silhouette seems to have been entrusted. No stranger to the supernatural world, she was like a favored child of Nature who appeared to have loosed her girdle, revealing all the caprice and charm and freedom lent to Beauty. She knew the slightest graces. Able to view such vast dimensions, she did not scorn to know the colors that tint the wings of butterflies or to study the symmetrical and marvelous network of fern spread like a canopy over the wild strawberry plant. She willingly listened to the murmuring streams in marshy fields where the hissing of the *love adder* is heard. She followed the dartings of the will-o'-the-wisps on the edge of meadows and fens, and imagined the visionary abodes toward which their flittings mislead the lagging traveler. She had heard the concerts droned by the cicada and its friends in the stubble of the fields, and had learned the names of dwellers in the winged republic of the woods, identifying them as skillfully by their plumaged dress as by their bantering roulades or plaintive cries. She knew all the softness of the lily's shades and the resplendence of its color, and she knew, too, all the despair of Geneviève,[3] the maiden enamored of flowers.

In her dreams she was visited by those unknown friends who came to join her "when she was despondent on a deserted bench." They were borne in "a large and laden bark afloat on a rapid stream" and she rushed aboard to leave for unfamiliar shores, "that land of fancy where the life of reality seems a misty dream to those who have yearned from childhood for great pearly shells; the ascendant course leads to isles where all are young and beautiful, the men and women crowned with flowers, hair floating on their shoulders, holding cups and harps that are strange in shape, with songs and voices that are not of this world, and each with an equal and wholly divine love for the other; where perfumed fountains play in silver basins, blue roses grow in Chinese vases, where the views are enchanting, where, with unshod feet, they tread on moss as smooth as velvet carpet, and run and sing in roaming through the balmy thickets."[4]

She knew these unknown friends so well that after their appearance she "could not think of them without trembling the live-long day. . . ." She who had surprised such ineffable smiles on the portraits of the dead was at home in this Hoffmannesque world.[5] She had noticed on what heads the sun's rays fell, forming a halo as they dropped from the height of some Gothic window like an

3. *André* [1835].
4. *Lettres d'un voyageur.*
5. *Spiridion* [1839].

arm of God, bright and intangible and surrounded by a swirl of atoms. She had recognized the splendid phantoms, clothed in gold and purple and the glory of the setting sun. The fantastic had no myth whose secret she did not share.

She was anxious to know him who had swiftly darted "toward those regions which elude description, but which must exist somewhere on earth or on some planet that sheds a lovely light to be seen in the woods at moonset."[6] He wished no more to leave those regions or ever to turn his heart and mind back to this world, so like to Finland's shores, where the mud and mire can be avoided only by climbing the naked granite of solitary rocks. Wearied by the burdensome vision she had called *Lélia,* wearied from dreaming of the grandly impossible kneaded with earthly materials, she was eager to know that artist who was *lover of an impossible,* so misty and bordering on the lands beyond the moon! But alas! if those lands are free of the miasma of our atmosphere, they do not escape our saddest desolations. Those who go there see suns that are alight, but others that are fading. The noblest stars of the Pleiades there vanish. Stars fall like drops of shining dew into nothingness, its gaping chasm not even perceived, and the soul, watching these ethereal savannas, this blue Sahara with shifting and perishing oases, becomes accustomed to a melancholy unbroken by either enthusiasm or admiration. Unstirred, it swallows and absorbs them. It is like the sleeping waters of a lake, its surface reflecting the outline and vibrations of the shore while its torpor stays un-

6. *Lettres d'un voyageur.*

changed. This sadness subdues even the merry bubblings of happiness "through exhaustion that is tied to tension of the soul lifted above the region that it naturally dwells in; . . . it demonstrates the inadequacy of human speech for the first time to those who have studied it so much and used it so well. . . . It carries far from all active and, so to say, militant instincts . . . sweeping out into space and reckless coursing, becoming lost in the vastness high above the clouds . . . where earth looks beautiful no longer, for only the sky is seen, . . . where reality is no more viewed with the poetic feeling of the author of *Waverly*, but where, the poem itself idealized, the infinite is peopled with its own creations after the manner of *Manfred*."[7]

Did Mme Sand sense that omnipresent sadness and obtrusive will, that invincible exclusiveness which underlies the habit of contemplation and controls the imagination given to indulgence in dreams bearing no resemblance to the surrounding world? Did she sense the form assumed by the deepest affection and complete devotion as they become synonymous with love? In order to sift early the mystery of these intense personalities, an instinctive reserve is essential, certainly in some respects. They withdraw into themselves as readily as those flowers that fold their petals before the least attacking wind, to unfurl them only in the rays of a kindly sun. Such natures are called *rich through exclusion* in contrast to those who are *rich in profusion*. "If they meet and mingle, they cannot fuse together," adds our oft-quoted novelist, "one must con-

7. *Lucrezia Floriani*. Identified in the 2nd edition.—*Trans.*

sume the other and leave only ashes behind!" Ah! there
are natures like that of the frail musician, whose days we
recall, that die in self-consumption, unwilling and unable
to live but a single life restricted to the demands of *their
own* ideal.

Chopin seemed to fear this woman more than other
women. Like a Delphic priestess she said so many things
that others could not say. He avoided her and delayed their
meeting. Because of her charming naturalness, one of her
noblest attractions, Mme Sand was unaware of this and
did not suspect his innocent shyness. She came before him,
and as he gazed upon her his prejudice against female authors, till then so stubbornly nurtured, quickly vanished.

In the fall of 1837 Chopin experienced worrisome
attacks of an ailment that robbed him of half his strength.
Alarming symptoms forced him to go south to escape the
harshness of winter. Mme Sand, always watchful and compassionate when her friends were ill, did not want him to
start out alone since his condition demanded care, and
she decided to go with him. They chose to go to the
island of Majorca where the sea air and constantly mild
climate are especially beneficial to patients afflicted by dis-
orders of the chest. Although he was so wasted when he
left that his return was not expected, and although he was
long and painfully ill, he recovered there sufficiently to
enjoy improved health for several years.

Was it only the climate that summoned him back to
life? Did not life itself hold him by its superlative fascination? Perhaps he lived because he willed to live, for the
rights of the will over our body—who knows their limita-

tion? Who knows what inward essence the will can loosen to save the body from collapse, what strength it can infuse into weakened organs? Who knows, indeed, the extent of the mind's dominion over matter? In how many things does our imagination govern our senses, double their sharpness or hasten their extinction, as it exerts its sway harshly and at length or suddenly merges forgotten energies to concentrate them in a single effort? When all the sun's prismatic rays are collected on the focal point of crystal, does not this fragile glass ignite a flame of celestial origin?

All the prismatic rays of happiness collected in that period of Chopin's life. Is it surprising that they re-enflamed his life and that it then burned with brightest effect? That solitude, amidst the Mediterranean's blue waves and the lime tree's shade, seemed by its location to fulfill the eager wish of youthful souls still hoping in their most innocent and blissful illusions and sighing for happiness *on a desert isle!* There he breathed that air which brings to exiled beings cruel nostalgia, that air which is all-pervasive and never met with except as others breathe it with us, the air of imagined countries which, in spite of all realities and obstacles, are so easily discovered when sought with another—the air of that ideal land whither we would take what we cherish, repeating with Mignon: *Dahin! Dahin! . . . lass' uns ziehn!* [Thither let us wend our way].

Throughout his illness Mme Sand never left his bedside for a moment. He loved her till the day of his death, with an affection that lost none of its intensity though its joyfulness disappeared, unswervingly loyal though bitten with pain—"for it seems that this delicate being was absorbed and consumed in the glow of his admiration. . . . Others seek happiness in their passions: when they find it no more these feelings gently steal away. In this they resemble everyone else, but he loved for the sake of loving. No suffering could dishearten him. He could enter a new phase, woefulness for instance, after exhausting that of rapture, but the mood of coldness never seized him. That would have been sheer physical agony, for his passion had become his life and, blissful or bitter, he was no longer free to escape it for a single moment."[8] From that time onward, indeed, Mme Sand never ceased being for Chopin the woman of supernatural power who had forced back death's shadows, who had transformed his sufferings into cherished languors.

To save him and snatch him away from such an early end, she bravely combatted his illness. She lavished upon him those intuitive and instinctive attentions which are often more effective than the remedies of science. As she watched over him she knew no weariness, no dejection, no boredom. Neither her strength nor her spirit wavered from the charge. She was like those sturdily healthy mothers that seem to transfer magnetically some of their strength to children who are ailing and who, ever clamoring for attention, also have their favorites. Finally the disease retreated and "the gloomy obsession that was secretly gnawing at Chopin's mind, corroding all peaceful contentment, slowly disappeared. He allowed his friend's

8. *Lucrezia Floriani*. Identified in the 2nd edition.—*Trans.*

easy nature and engaging serenity to banish the sad thoughts and mournful forebodings and to bolster his mental well-being."[9]

Happiness followed gloomy fear like the steady triumphal development of a lovely day succeeding a dark night packed with terror. At first the arching shadows weigh so heavily that a near and final catastrophe seems impending, with escape unthought of, then the despairing eye suddenly sights a point where these shadows part like cottony fluff, its thickness rent by a tearing hand. The first ray of hope now pierces the soul. Breathing is freer, as with those who, lost in a darkened cavern, glimpse a light that is far from certain! This wavering light is the opening dawn, projecting such vague hues that they recall the fall of eve or the close of dusk. But daybreak is proclaimed by freshened winds which, like harbingers, bring a message of salvation in their pure and vital breezes. An arborescent balm permeates the air like the quickening of hope, encouraged and strengthened. A bird of morning, perchance, sings his happy lay, which resounds in the heart like a first and calm awaking, proffered as an omen of the future. Scarce-noticed but undoubted signs persuade, as they increase, that in this struggle between shadow and light, between death and life, night's sorrows must be vanquished. The oppression slackens. The gaze is directed toward the leaden sky, and it seems to weigh less fatally. It has lost its frightful fixity.

The grayish streaks increase little by little and stretch across the horizon like narrow bands on the verge of open-

9. *Lucrezia Floriani*. Identified in the 2nd edition.—*Trans.*

ing. They forthwith widen, exceed their borders, and, like the surface of a flooding pond, overflow its parched banks in uncontrolled splashes. Sharp opposition arises, dikes seem to abound to halt the advance of light, and clouds seem to assemble like drifting sand. But like the irresistible wrath of roaring waters, the light smashes, destroys, and devours them, and as it ascends, waves of purple give it a reddish tinge. At that moment it glows with a shy and conquering grace, and its innocent sweetness makes the knee bend in gratitude. The final terror has vanished. Rebirth is at hand!

Then objects surge into view as if rising out of nothingness. A rose-colored veil seems to hide them until the light grows more intense. Its delicate drapery here and there shades into palish pink, while the foreground brightens in a white and dazzling reflection.

The shining sun invades the heavens. The higher it rises, the more brilliance it sheds. Mists collect and roll from right to left like billowing curtains. Then all things breathe and live, stir, shout and sing; sounds commingle and merge, clash and fuse. Inertia yields to motion, which swirls and spreads and speeds its way. The waves of the lake are swollen like a breast surcharged with love. Teardrops of dew, aquiver like tears of compassion, become ever clearer, and they successively sparkle on the moistened grasses like diamonds waiting for the sun to come and paint their flashings. In the east the enormous fan of light unfolds ever wide and vaster. Streamers of gold, spangles of silver, fringes of violet, and borders of scarlet cover it with their huge embroidery. Reflections of bronze adorn its panels. In its center a more vivid carmine assumes the transparency of ruby, shades into orange like a glowing ember, flares out like a torch, and flowers at last like a bouquet of flames rising ever higher, ever hotter, ever more incandescent.

At last the god of day appears! His luminous hair sets off his dazzling brow. He mounts slowly; but scarcely has he fully revealed himself than he dashes on, rids himself of all that surrounds him, leaves earth far below, and instantaneously takes possession of the heavens.

The memory of the days passed on the island of Majorca remained a delight in Chopin's heart, an ecstasy that fate grants only once to her most favored. "He was no longer bound to earth, he was in an empyrean of perfumes and golden clouds; he seemed to immerse his imagination, so refined and lovely, in a monologue with the very Deity, and if occasionally over the radiant prism, where he lost all thought of self, some incident obtruded the trifling magic lantern of the world, he sensed a frightful unease. It was as if, in the midst of a sublime concert, a screeching hurdy-gurdy were mingling its shrill tones and a vulgar musical theme with the divine thoughts of great masters."[10] Still deeply grateful, he subsequently spoke of this period as of one of life's blessings that make for happiness. He had no hope that it would ever be possible to find again a felicity in which the tenderness of woman and the flashes of genius successively mark the passage of time—like the clock of flowers that Linnaeus had created in his hothouses in Uppsala to tell the hours by their successive bloomings,

10. *Lucrezia Floriani.* Identified in the 2nd edition.—*Trans.*

a rhythmical exhaling of varied perfumes, and a disclosure of other beauties as their manifold calyxes opened outward.

The magnificent lands that the poet and the musician crossed together were impressed more clearly on the former's imagination. The beauties of nature reacted on Chopin less sharply though not less strongly. His soul was moved thereby and felt at once in harmony with their grandeur and enchantment, but his mind was under no compulsion to analyze or define them, to classify or name them. His soul trembled in unison with impressive landscapes, but he could not at the moment associate the source of the phenomenon with each sensation. Like a true musician he was content to seize upon and, so to say, extract the feeling of the scenes he viewed, seemingly inattentive to the plastic aspect and picturesque frame which would not merge with the medium of his art and did not belong to his more spiritualized sphere. And yet (an effect frequently noticed in such beings) the more distant he was from times and scenes when emotion had dulled his senses, as the clouds of incense obscure the censer, the more the shapes and outlines of these places and situations seemed to gain clarity in his eyes. In ensuing years he spoke most charmingly of these memories. But when he was so fully happy he took no account of his happiness. He let it embrace him, as we all do in our tenderest years of childhood, submitting to the influence of nature with no realization of it and then discovering solely in our memory the exact picture of every object that we can describe only long after we cease to see it.

Moreover, why should he have cast an observant eye over the beauties of Spain, which formed the setting of his poetic happiness? Did he not find them still more beautiful as portrayed by the inspired word of his traveling companion? He saw these delightful spots a second time through the palette of her impassioned genius, as through red-stained windows all objects and the atmosphere itself appear to be dyed in raging flame. Was this wonderful nurse not a great artist? Rare and marvelous union! If nature, endowing a woman, joined the most brilliant gifts of the mind to those depths of tenderness and devotion where lies embedded her true and irresistible power—without which she is no more than an answerless riddle—the flames of imagination, mingling with the limpid purity of the heart, would somehow renew the miraculous spectacle of ancient Greek fire. Its brilliant blaze would skim the trough of the sea and not be extinguished, adding in the waves' reflection the richness of purple to the celestial beauty of blue.

Is it possible for genius to attain the humblest splendors of the heart, those limitless sacrifices of past and future, those immolations as brave as they are inexplicable, those surrenderings of self, not transient and changing but constant and persistent, which entitle tenderness to be called devotion? Does not the power of genius have rightful demands, and the rightful power of woman—is it not to renounce all demands? Can the royal purple and the burning flames of genius float on the stainless azure of a woman's destiny?

8

ILLNESS AND DEATH—EPILOGUE

*C*HOPIN'S HEALTH, passing through various stages, declined steadily from 1840 on. For some years the weeks that he spent each summer in the region of Nohant gave him his best moments. He seemed to find more relaxation there than elsewhere. Since he worked there with pleasure, he returned each year with several compositions, but the winters brought on a gradual intensification of suffering. At first, movement became difficult for him, and soon wellnigh impossible. From 1846 to 1847 he scarcely walked any more and was unable to climb stairs without painful gasping. Thereafter he lived only by dint of care and precaution.

Toward the spring of 1847 his condition, worsening from day to day, developed into an illness from which he was not expected to recover. Once more he was saved, but this period was marked by a catastrophe so heart-rending that he promptly termed it mortal. Indeed, he did not long survive the rupture of his friendship with Mme Sand that then occurred. Mme de Staël, generous and warm of heart, fine and quick of mind, who had the fault of often dulling her words with pedantry that robbed them of easy freedom, said, on one of those days when her bubbling emotion loosened her from the formality of her Genevan stiffness: "In love there are only beginnings!" an exclamation, born of bitter experience, on the inadequacy of the human heart to accomplish all the beautiful dreams of the imagination. Ah! if there were no examples of blessed sublimeness to belie at times so many known and unknown deeds that seem to strengthen Mme de Staël's phrase, every one of us would succumb to disbelief and disavowal in the face of showers of affection. We should imagine that we saw the allegoric figure in the ancient procession of the lovely canephorei who carry flowers only to enhance the beauty of a victim!

Chopin often spoke then of Mme Sand, and almost fondly; there was no bitterness, no recrimination. Tears would come to his eyes when he uttered her name, but he abandoned himself to a kind of torturing sweetness in the remembered ardor of former days, now bereft of their radiant meaning. In spite of the subterfuges that his friends employed to remove this subject from his memory and to escape its upsetting power, he liked to dwell upon it as if he wished to ruin his life through the same feelings that had formerly cheered it and to smother himself in this fatal balm. To indulge himself in observing the final collapse of his final hopes was his final pleasure. Vainly did they attempt to draw his mind elsewhere. He always spoke of it, and when he spoke of it no more, was it not still in his thought? He seemed to inhale the poison greedily as if to breathe it for a shorter time.

However limited the number of days that his physical weakness promised, the painful sufferings that ended them should have been spared him. Both tender and warm of soul, but demanding in his refinements and aversions, he was content to live only among the shining phantoms that he could evoke and the lofty griefs that he sheltered in his breast. He was one victim the more—and a noble, illustrious victim—of the momentary attractions of two natures, contrasting in character, who suddenly meet and experience a delightful astonishment. They assume this to be a lasting emotion, and accordingly they form illusions and promises that they cannot fulfill. When the dream is over, that nature which is the most deeply impressed and the most firm in its hopes and affections (and which could never shift them elsewhere) is the one that is shattered and wasted. A terrible faculty emanating from man's most beautiful endowments! They carry in their train flames and devastation, like the chargers of the sun when Phaëthon, his hand become slack, fails to hold them to their beneficent course and lets them wander at will, upsetting the heavenly system.

Chopin felt and often repeated that when this bond, this long friendship was broken, his life was broken, too.

During that illness, his life was despaired of for several

days. M. Gutmann, his most distinguished pupil and the friend admitted to his closest intimacy in those last years, lavished upon him evidence of his affection. His care and his company were the most satisfying, and when Princess Czartoryska came, visiting him every day and more than once fearing not to find him on the morrow, Chopin would ask her, with the shy timidity of the ill and with a tender delicacy that was peculiarly his own: "Whether Gutmann was not very weary? Whether he would watch over him still, for his presence was sweeter to him than any other's." His convalescence was very slow and painful, and it restored no more than a breath of life. He changed at this time so much that he became scarcely recognizable.

The following summer brought him that questionable improvement that the lovely season grants to persons who are dying. He would not leave Paris, and thus refused the pure country air and its invigorating benefits.

The winter 1847–1848 was nothing but a painful and ceaseless alternation of relief and relapse. In the spring, however, he resolved to accomplish his old project of going to London. When the February revolution broke out, he was still in bed. With melancholy effort he seemed to try to take an interest in current events, and he spoke of them more than was his wont. M. Gutmann continued to be his closest intimate and his most constant visitor. His were the attentions that Chopin preferred to the very end.

In April, finding his health improved, he thought of making his trip to visit that country which was his destination when youth and life still offered their happiest prospects. He set out for England where his works had already encountered an intelligent public and were generally known and admired.[1] He left France in that frame of mind

1. For several years Chopin's compositions were already very widely known and much appreciated in England. The best virtuosos performed them frequently. In a brochure entitled *An Essay on the Works of F. Chopin*, published in London by Wessel and Stappleton, we find some highly appropriate lines. The motto of this little pamphlet is cleverly chosen, and Shelley's two verses (from *Peter Bell the Third*) could not be better applied than to Chopin:

> He was a mighty poet—and
> A subtle-souled psychologist.

The author of the pages mentioned speaks enthusiastically of that "originative genius untrammeled by conventionalities, unfettered by pedantry . . ."; of those "outpourings of an unworldly and trustful soul—those floods of tears, and gushes of pure joyfulness, those exquisite embodiments of fugitive thoughts, those infinitesimal delicacies," which give so much value to Chopin's slightest sketches. Later the English author says: "One thing is certain, viz: to play with proper feeling and correct execution, the *Préludes* and *Studies* of Chopin, is to be neither more nor less than a finished pianist, and moreover, to comprehend them thoroughly, to give a life and a tongue to their infinite and most eloquent subtleties of expression, involves the necessity of being in no less a degree a poet than a pianist, a thinker than a musician. Commonplace is instinctively avoided in all the works of Chopin; a stale cadence or a trite progression, a hum-drum subject or a hackneyed sequence, a vulgar twist of the melody or a worn-out passage, a meagre harmony or an unskilful counterpoint, may in vain be looked for throughout the entire range of his compositions, the prevailing characteristics of which, are, a feeling, as uncommon as beautiful, a treatment as original as felicitous, a melody and a harmony, as new, fresh, vigorous, and striking as they are utterly unexpected, and out of the ordinary track. In taking up one of the works of Chopin, you are entering, as it were, a fairy land, untrodden by human footsteps, a path, hitherto unfrequented, but by the great composer himself; and a faith, and a devotion, *a desire to appreciate, and a determination to understand*, are absolutely necessary, to do it anything like adequate justice . . . Chopin in his *Polonaises* and in his *Mazoures* has aimed at those characteristics,

that the English call *low spirits*. The momentary interest
that he strove to take in political changes had soon vanished. He had become more silent than ever. If a few
words absent-mindedly escaped him, they were only an utterance of regret. His affection for the small number of
persons he continued to see took on the heart-rending hues
of emotions before last farewells. His attitude of indifference obviously extended to other matters as well. Art alone
retained its power over him. In those moments, growing
ever shorter, when he could be concerned with it, he gave
himself as ardently to music as in the days when he was
filled with life and hope. Before leaving Paris he gave a
concert there in the halls of M. Pleyel, one of the friends
with whom his relations were most frequent, constant, and
warm. He is now paying worthy homage to his memory
and friendship by zealously and actively working for the
creation of a monument for his tomb. At this concert
Chopin's public, as select as it was faithful, heard him for
the last time.

He was welcomed to London with an eagerness that
helped him shake off his sadness and dispel his dejection.
Perhaps he thought he would succeed in vanquishing them
in forgetfulness, even including his habits of the past. He

---

which distinguish the national music of his country so markedly
from that of all others, that quaint idiosyncrasy, that identical
wildness and fantasticality, that delicious mingling of the sad and
the cheerful, which invariably and forcibly individualize the music
of those northern countries, whose language delights, in combi-
nation of consonants . . ."

[The quotations in this footnote are in English in the first
edition.—*Trans.*]

neglected the prescriptions of doctors and the precautions that reminded him of his feeble condition. He played in public twice, and many times in private gatherings. He mingled much in society, kept late hours, and risked every fatigue. He was not to be daunted by any consideration of health.

In the home of the Duchess of Sutherland he was presented to the Queen, and the most distinguished salons sought the pleasure of entertaining him. He left for Edinburgh, where the climate was especially harmful. Returning from Scotland, he was greatly weakened. The doctors urged him to quit England as soon as possible, but he put off his departure for some time. Who could tell the feeling that caused this delay? He played at one more concert that was given for Poles—a final expression of love extended to his country, a final glance, a final sigh, and a final sorrow! He was fêted, applauded, and surrounded by all his countrymen. He bade them all a farewell which they did not think would be forever. What thoughts filled his mind as he crossed the sea returning to Paris—that Paris which was so different for him from the one he had found, without seeking it, in 1831?

Entering the city this time, he was surprised by a blow as keen as it was unexpected. Dr. Molin was dying—the physician whose advice and sensible guidance had already saved his life in the winter of 1847, and to whom alone, Chopin believed, he owed his continued existence for many years. This death was more than a painful loss. It ushered in such a doomful despondency, in those intervals when the attitude of mind exerts so much control over the course of the disease, that he became convinced that no one could replace Molin's attentions. He had no further confidence in any doctor. Henceforth he constantly went from one to another, dissatisfied with all and without hope in their knowledge. He succumbed to a kind of superstitious depression. No bond stronger than life, no love as strong as death appeared to combat this bitter apathy.

From the winter of 1848 Chopin was no longer able to work continuously. From time to time he retouched a few leaves of sketches, but failed to develop their ideas. Honestly mindful of his fame, he wanted to see them burned in order to prevent their being garbled, mutilated, and changed into posthumous works unworthy of him.

The only completed manuscripts he left, like shreds of memory, were a final *Nocturne* and a very short *Valse*. Last of all he had planned to write a piano method in which he expected to sum up his ideas on the theory and technic of his art, offering the harvest of his long industry, his happy innovations, and his comprehending experience. It was a heavy responsibility and required redoubled application even from as diligent a worker as Chopin. By taking shelter in these barren regions he wished, perhaps, to avoid the very emotions of art, which assumes such different forms from the heart's sereneness and loneliness! He sought only a single and consuming occupation, he asked of it only what Manfred vainly asked of the powers of magic: *Forgetfulness!* Forgetfulness—which is granted by neither diversion nor benumbedness. On the contrary, filled with envenomed craftiness, they seem to pay back in intensity the moments they have snatched from grief. In that daily labor which "allays the storms of the soul" [*der Seele Sturm beschwört*], he doubtless wished to find forgetfulness, only occasionally achieved, by stifling the memory when he did not efface it. A poet, also the prey of inconsolable sadness, while awaiting early death, sought likewise to assuage these depressing sorrows in labor, and he invokes it as a last recourse against life's bitterness at the end of that virile elegy he called *The Ideal:*

> *Beschäftigung, die nie ermattet,*
> *Die langsam schafft, doch nie zerstört,*
> *Die zu dem Bau der Ewigkeiten*
> *Zwar Sandkorn nur für Sandkorn reicht,*
> *Doch von der grossen Schlud der Zeiten,*
> *Minuten, Tage, Jahre streicht.*[2]

But Chopin's energies no longer sufficed for his plans. This task was too abstract and too tiring. He dwelt mentally upon the form of his project, and mentioned it at different times, yet it was impossible to realize. He jotted down only a few pages, which were destroyed with the rest.

At last the illness increased so obviously that the fears of his friends began to wax desperate. Soon he left his bed

2. Schiller, *Die Ideale.*
   [Employment—thou, the never-tiring,
   Who toilsome shap'st, nor break'st the form!
   Eternity's huge pile—increasing,
   As grain on grain the fabric rears,
   And, from Time's mighty debt, unceasing,
   Still striking minutes, days and years!
   —Tr. John Herman Merivale.]

no more and scarcely spoke more. Receiving this news, his sister came from Warsaw, stationed herself beside his bed, and remained there. He saw around him anguish and portents and redoubled sadness, and he gave no sign of what he witnessed. He talked of his death with a calmness and a resignation that were truly Christian, yet he did not stop providing for the morrow. The liking he always had for change of residence appeared once more. He took another lodging, arranged its furnishings anew, and busied himself with minute details. Since he had not countermanded the arrangements for moving in, the removal was promptly begun, and it happened that on the very day of his death his furniture was carried to the apartment he was not to occupy.

Did he fear that death would not fulfill its promise, that, having brushed him with its finger it might once more leave him in the world? Did he fear that life would be more cruel if he had to resume it after breaking all its ties? Did he feel that double influence that affects certain gifted beings on the eve of events deciding their fate, that glaring contradiction between the heart besieging the secret of the future and the mind that dares not glimpse it? There is an opposition between simultaneous anticipations which at certain moments implants in the firmest minds counsels that their deeds seem to belie, and yet they flow from equal urgings.

From week to week, soon from day to day, death's shadow appeared more heavy. The illness was approaching its end; the suffering was becoming more severe; the crises grew more frequent, and each one brought the final agony closer. When they relaxed, and to the end, Chopin regained his presence of mind and vital will. He lost neither lucidness of thought nor clarity of purpose. The wishes he expressed in moments of respite attest the solemn calmness in which he watched his end draw near. He wished to be buried beside Bellini with whom he had had frequent and friendly relations during the latter's stay in Paris. Bellini's tomb is located in the cemetery of Père-Lachaise, next to that of Cherubini. The desire to know this great master (in whose admiration he had been raised) was one of the reasons, as he traveled from Vienna to London in 1831, which led Chopin to go through Paris, where he had no idea that fate would hold him. Now he lies between Bellini and Cherubini, such different geniuses. Yet Chopin approaches both in equal degree, valuing the science of one as much as sensing sympathy for the other. Like the author of *Norma* he inhaled the feeling for melody, but he aspired to the harmonic depth and substance of the learned elder. He wished to combine in a grand and lofty way the misty vagueness of spontaneous emotion with the skills of consummate masters.

Maintaining his reserve to the end, he asked to see no one for the last time, but a shining, touching gratefulness was in the thanks addressed to friends who visited him. The first days of October left no further doubt or hope. The fatal time drew nigh; no more could the following day or hour be counted. His sister and Gutmann were with him constantly and did not leave him for a second. The Countess Delphine Potocka, absent from Paris, returned when she learned that the danger was imminent. Those who came close to the dying man, one and all, could not tear themselves from the sight of this great and lovely soul in this supreme moment.

However violent or frivolous the passions are that stir the heart, whatever strength or indifference they release in face of sudden and unlooked-for accidents which would seem to be the most overwhelming, the sight of a slow and beautiful death has an imposing majesty which moves and attracts, softens and uplifts souls that are least prepared for this holy contemplation. The slow and lingering departure of one among us for the shores of the unknown, the mysterious gravity of his secret dreams and of his commemoration of thoughts and deeds on the narrow threshold separating past from future shakes us more profoundly than anything else in the world. Catastrophes, abysses that the earth opens beneath our feet, conflagrations enwrapping whole cities in flaming sheaths, the terrible possibilities facing a fragile ship which the tempest turns into a toy, blood drawn by weapons and mixed with the direful smoke of battle, the fearsome charnel house itself which a contagious plague makes of our homes—these put us less appreciably beyond the reach of sordid influences, which pass and tire and break [*qui passent, qui lassent et qui cassent*], than the prolonged view of a conscious soul silently watching the multiform aspects of time and the mute door of eternity. Courage and resignation, nobility and emotion, acquainting the soul with the inevitable dissolution so hostile to our instincts, impress witnesses more profoundly than the most frightful vicissitudes since they rob the scene of its heartbreak and reflection.

In the salon adjoining Chopin's bedroom a few persons were constantly together. They approached him in turn to receive a gesture and a glance for want of his failing word. On Sunday, October 15, crises still more painful than earlier ones lasted several hours. He bore them patiently and with great spiritual fortitude. The Countess Delphine Potocka, who was then present, was deeply affected and wept. He noticed her standing at the foot of his bed, tall, slender, clothed in white, and resembling the most angelic figures that the most devout painters could envision. Doubtless he thought this was some heavenly apparition, and as the attack left him a moment of relief he asked her to sing. He was thought at first to be delirious, but he earnestly repeated his request. Who would have dared oppose it? The piano was rolled from the salon to the door of the bedroom, and the Countess sang, her voice choked in sobs and with tears streaming down her cheeks. Never before, surely, had this exquisite talent and wondrous voice achieved an expression so filled with pathos. Chopin seemed to suffer less while he listened. She sang the famous Hymn to the Virgin which, it is said, had saved the life of Stradella. "How beautiful it is! My God, how beautiful!" he exclaimed, "Again—again!" Although overcome by emotion, the Countess had the noble courage to grant this final wish of a friend and compatriot. She reseated herself at the piano and sang a Psalm of Marcello. Chopin was worse, everyone was frightened. Spontaneously the entire company knelt, no one ventured to speak, and only the voice of the Countess was heard, soaring like a celestial melody above the sighs and sobs that served as its muffled and mournful accompaniment. Night was falling. A semi-darkness lent its mysterious shadows to this sad scene. Chopin's sister, prostrate near his bed, wept and prayed, and she scarcely changed this position as long as her cherished brother remained alive.

During the night the patient's condition worsened, but improved Monday morning. As if he had known in advance the appointed and propitious moment, he promptly requested the last sacraments. In the absence of Abbé ——, to whom he was closely bound in common exile, he summoned Abbé Alexandre Jelowicki, one of the most distinguished men among the Polish emigrants. He saw him twice. When the holy viaticum was administered, he received it with deep devotion in the presence of his friends. Shortly after, he had them approach his bed, one by one, to give each of them a final blessing, and he asked that God's grace be upon them, their affections, and their hopes. All knees bent, all heads bowed; eyes were moist, and hearts were heavy and uplifted.

Still more painful crises occurred and continued throughout the day. The night from Monday to Tuesday he spoke not a word and seemed no longer to distinguish the persons around him. Only in the evening, about eleven o'clock, did he feel relief. Abbé Jelowicki had not left him.

Hardly had he recovered speech than he wished to recite with the Abbé the prayers and litanies of the dying. He did this in Latin, his voice loud and clear. From this moment on he leaned his head constantly on the shoulder of Gutmann who, during the course of the illness, had devoted to him his days and his nights.

A convulsive drowsiness lasted until October 17, 1849. The death struggle began about two o'clock. Cold sweat flowed copiously on his forehead. After a short spell of dozing he asked, in a barely audible voice: "Who is near me?" He lowered his head to kiss Gutmann's hand, which was holding him, and yielded up his soul in this final proof of friendship and gratitude. He died as he had lived—in loving!

When the doors of the salon opened, his lifeless body was instantly surrounded, and it was long before the tears ceased to flow from those about him.

Since his fondness for flowers was well known, such a quantity arrived the next day that the bed on which he lay and the very room itself vanished beneath their different colors. He seemed to rest in a garden. His face resumed a youthfulness, a purity, and an unaccustomed serenity. His young beauty, so long clouded over by suffering, reappeared. M. Clesinger reproduced those charming features, their original grace restored by death, in a sketch which he immediately fashioned and then executed in marble for his tomb.

Chopin's devout admiration for the genius of Mozart led him to request the performance of his *Requiem* at his obsequies. This wish was fulfilled. The ceremony took place in the Madeleine, October 30, 1849, delayed this long so that the performance of this great work would be worthy of master and disciple. The foremost artists of Paris wished to take part. At the Introit Chopin's *Funeral March* was heard, orchestrated for this occasion by M. Reber, and for the Offertory M. Lefébure-Wély played his wonderful *Preludes* in B minor and E minor on the organ. The solo parts of the *Requiem* were claimed by Mme Viardot and Mme Castellan; and M. Lablache, who had sung the *Tuba mirum* from the same *Requiem* in 1827 at Beethoven's burial, now sang it again. M. Meyerbeer, who then had played the timpani, led the mourning procession with Prince Adam Czartoryski. The pallbearers were Prince Alexandre Czartoryski, M. Delacroix, M. Franchomme, and M. Gutmann.

However inadequate these pages are to discuss Chopin as we should wish, we hope that the appeal his name so rightly exerts will supply all that is lacking. If it were incumbent upon us to add a few words to these lines—stamped as they are with the memory of his works and of all he held dear, and possibly made eloquent and sympathetic only through the truth of deeply felt sorrow, esteem, and enthusiasm—words forced upon us by inevitable reflection as each death removes a man's companions of youth and shatters the ties first formed by his confiding and deluded heart (the pain the more grievous if they were strong enough to survive that youth)—we should say that within one year we lost the two most precious friends we met during our career of wandering. One fell in combat in the civil wars! Valiant and ill-fated hero, he was victim of a frightful death, but not for a moment could its horrible tortures dent his fiery courage, his fearless composure, his knightly daring. A young prince, rarely intelligent and prodigiously active, his spirit hot and bubbling like a volatile gas, endowed with outstanding skills, he had no more than succeeded in conquering difficulties through his tireless energy and in creating an arena where his abilities could be utilized as successfully in jousts of eloquence and manipulation of affairs as in his brilliant feats of arms. The other was slowly consumed in his own flames. His life, excluded from public phenomena, was incorporeal, and we find it revealed only in the evidence left by his songs. He ended his days in a foreign land which was never his adopted country; he was faithful to the eternal widowhood of his own. He was the poet of the stricken soul, with its secrets, silences, and sorrowing fears.

The death of Prince Felix Lichnowsky terminated the immediate interest we could feel in the activity of groups he was connected with. Chopin's death snatched away the compensations inherent in an all-embracing friendship. The affectionate sympathy for our ways of feeling and our approach to art, of which so many unquestioned proofs were given by this reserved artist, would have softened the disappointments and strains that still await us, just as they encourage and strengthened our early inclinations and early attempts.

Since it is our lot to survive them, we should like at least to express the sorrow we experience, and we felt impelled to lay homage of our grieving respect upon the tomb of the remarkable musician who passed among us. Today, when music is developing so widely and magnificently, we are reminded in some ways of the painters of the fourteenth and fifteenth centuries. They compressed the productions of their genius onto the margins of parchment, but they painted their miniatures with evidence of such happy inspiration that, being the first to break Byzantine stiffness, they bequeathed the most delightful models, and the Francias and Peruginos and Raphaels of the future had to transfer them later to canvas and fresco.

There have been peoples with the custom of forming pyramids to commemorate great men and great deeds. Each passer-by brought a stone to the mound, and it grew imperceptibly to an unforeseen height, the anonymous work of all. In our days monuments are still similarly erected; but, thanks to a happy union, instead of a rude and formless mass appearing, the participation of everyone assures a work of art which is destined not solely to perpetuate the mute memory of the honored. It also awakens in future ages, helped by the poetic chisel, those feelings that were experienced by contemporaries. This results from subscriptions opened for the purpose of raising magnificent statues and tombs for men who made their country and their time illustrious.

Immediately after Chopin's death, M. Camille Pleyel

conceived a plan of this type. He organized a subscription (as was anticipated, it quickly reached a considerable amount) with the aim of having executed for Père-Lachaise cemetery the marble statue modeled by M. Clesinger. For our part, in thinking of our long friendship for Chopin, of the exceptional admiration we held for him from his entry into the musical world; thinking that, artist like him, we have often been the interpreter of his inspirations and, we are bold to say, the interpreter he loved and favored; that we, more often than others, heard from his lips the details of his method; that we were somehow identified with his thoughts on art and with the sentiments that he confided to it in that long process of assimilation existing between a writer and his translator; we believed that these circumstances imposed on us a duty beyond the contribution of a crude and nameless stone in homage of the honored. We concluded that the claims of friendship and association demanded a more personal testimony of our living sorrow and firm admiration. It seemed to us that we should be self-betraying did we not court the honor of inscribing our name and proclaiming our affliction on his sepulchral stone, a privilege permitted to those who never hope to fill the emptiness of their heart after an irreparable loss!